HOW TO RUN A COUNTRY

HOW TO RUN A COUNTRY

■ ■ ■ ■ ■

An Ancient Guide for Modern Leaders

Marcus Tullius Cicero

*Selected, translated, and with an
introduction by Philip Freeman*

PRINCETON UNIVERSITY PRESS

PRINCETON AND OXFORD

Published by Princeton University Press, 41 William Street
Princeton, New Jersey 08540
In the United Kingdom: Princeton University Press, 6 Oxford Street,
Woodstock, Oxfordshire OX20 1TW

press.princeton.edu

Library of Congress Cataloging-in-Publication Data

Cicero, Marcus Tullius.
[Selections. English]
How to run a country : an ancient guide for modern leaders /
Marcus Tullius Cicero ; selected, translated, and with an introduction
by Philip Freeman.
p.   cm.
Includes bibliographical references.
ISBN 978-0-691-15657-6 (hardcover : alk. paper) 1. Cicero, Marcus
Tullius—Translations into English. 2. Cicero, Marcus Tullius—Political
and social views. 3. Political science—Early works to 1800.
4. Leadership—Early works to 1800. I. Freeman, Philip, 1961– II. Title.
PA6278.A3F74 2013
320—dc23   2012030811

British Library Cataloging-in-Publication Data is available

This book has been composed in Stempel Garamond and Futura

Printed on acid-free paper. ∞

Printed in the United States of America

3 5 7 9 10 8 6 4 2

CONTENTS

CONTENTS

INTRODUCTION

I seem to read the history of all ages and nations
in every page—and especially the history of our
country for forty years past. Change the names and
every anecdote will be applicable to us.

—John Adams on Middleton's *Life of Cicero*

Marcus Tullius Cicero was born in 106 BC, four
hundred years after Rome had expelled her last
king and established the Republic. Cicero was
from the small country town of Arpinum in the
hills southeast of Rome. It was also the home
of Gaius Marius, who had scandalized the aristocracy of the Roman senate with his populist
politics and reorganization of the army into a
volunteer force with no property qualifications
for service. When Cicero was still a toddler,

Marius saved Rome from an invasion by Germanic tribes from across the Alps and cemented his hold on political power.

Cicero's family was of modest means, but his father was determined to give Marcus and his younger brother Quintus the best education possible. The boys studied history, philosophy, and rhetoric in Rome with the finest teachers of the day. As a young man, Marcus served a short and undistinguished term in the army, after which he began his legal training in Rome. One of Cicero's first cases as a lawyer was defending a man named Roscius unjustly accused of killing his father. This put young Cicero at odds with Sulla, the Roman dictator at the time, and his corrupt administration. It was a brave act, and Roscius was acquitted, but when the trial was finished Cicero thought it best to remove himself from Rome to pursue his studies in Greece and Rhodes.

After Sulla died and Rome had returned to republican government, Cicero began his rise through the ranks of the magistrates from quaestor to praetor and at last, after a hard-won campaign, to the office of consul, the highest office in the Republic. But the country Cicero ruled over during his year in office was not the same one his ancestors had known. The small village on the banks of the Tiber River had grown to an empire stretching across the Mediterranean. The simple ways of heroes such as the fabled Cincinnatus, who returned to his plough after being called to lead his country in war, had given way to corruption and abuse at home and abroad. The citizen armies of years past had become professional soldiers loyal to their generals rather than the state. Sulla's march on Rome and the subsequent slaughter of his political opponents had set a terrible precedent that would never be forgotten. The bonds of constitutional government were coming apart even as Cicero rose to the heights of Roman power. To make matters worse, the political factions of the day refused to listen to each other, the economy was stagnating, and unemployment was an ongoing threat to civic stability.

During Cicero's term as consul, the disgruntled nobleman Catiline tried to violently overthrow the senate, only to be stopped by Cicero and his allies. But three years later Pompey, Crassus, and Julius Caesar formed a triumvirate to rule Rome behind the scenes. They invited Cicero to join them, but he wanted nothing to do with such an unconstitutional arrangement. Still, he owed a great deal to Pompey for his support over the years and was impressed with the promise of Caesar. Cicero bided his time, tried to maintain good relations with all parties, and waited for the return of his beloved Republic.

Marginalized in the senate and without real power, Cicero in frustration began to write about how a government should be run. As Caesar conquered Gaul, then crossed the Rubicon and plunged Rome into civil war, Cicero penned some of the greatest works of political philosophy in history. The questions he asked echo still today: What is the foundation of a just government? What kind of rule is best? How should a leader behave in office? Cicero addressed these and many other questions head-on, not as an academic theorist but as someone who had run a country himself and had seen with his own eyes the collapse of republican government. He wrote for anyone who would listen, but his political influence had markedly declined. As he wrote to a friend: "I used to sit on the deck and hold the rudder of the state in my hands; now there's scarcely room for me in the bilge."

Caesar's victory in the civil war and the beginning of his benevolent dictatorship seemed like the end of the world to Cicero. But the Ides of March in 44 BC gave birth to a new flurry of optimism as Cicero worked for the rebirth of republican government. He placed his hopes in young Octavian, Caesar's great-nephew and heir, believing he might restore Rome to its former glory. But Octavian's alliance with Mark Antony showed Cicero that power once gained is not easily set aside. Cicero's final attempt to restore the Republic was to turn his formidable oratorical talents against the tyranny of Antony — but the age of freedom had passed away. With Octavian's assent, Antony passed a death sentence on his nemesis. Cicero's last words were to the assassins who came for him: "At least make sure you cut off my head *properly*."

INTRODUCTION

Cicero was a prolific author who wrote many essays, treatises, and letters dealing with how to run a government. This short anthology can provide only a small sample of his ideas recorded over many years and under different circumstances. Hopefully it will inspire readers to explore further other surviving works of Rome's greatest statesman.

Cicero was a moderate conservative—an increasingly rare breed in our modern world—who believed in working with other parties for the good of his country and its people. Rather than a politician, his ideas are those of a statesman, another category whose ranks today grow ever more diminished.

Cicero's political writings are an invaluable source for the study of ancient Rome, but his insights and wisdom are timeless. The use and abuse of power has changed little in two thousand years. For those who will listen, Cicero still has important lessons to teach. Among these are:

1. *There are universal laws that govern the conduct of human affairs.* Cicero would never have thought of this concept of natural law in terms used later by Christians, but he firmly believed that divine rules independent of time and place guarantee fundamental freedoms to everyone and constrain the way in which governments should behave. As the American Founding Fathers, careful students of Cicero, wrote in the *Declaration of Independence*: "We hold these truths to be self-evident, that all men are created equal, that they are endowed by their Creator with certain unalienable rights, that among these are life, liberty and the pursuit of happiness."

2. *The best form of government embraces a balance of powers.* Even the most noble kings will become tyrants if their reign is unchecked, just as democracy will degrade into mob rule if there are no constraints on popular power. A just government must be founded on a system of checks and balances. Beware the leader who sets aside constitutional rules claiming the need for expediency or security.

3. *Leaders should be of exceptional character and integrity.* Those who would govern a country must possess great courage, ability, and resolve. True leaders always put the interest of their nation above their own. As Cicero says, governing a country is like steering a ship, especially when the storm winds begin to blow. If the captain is not able to hold a steady course, the voyage will end in disaster for all.

4. *Keep your friends close—and your enemies closer*. Leaders fail when they take their friends and allies for granted. Never neglect your supporters, but even more important, always make sure you know what your enemies are doing. Don't be afraid to reach out to those who oppose you. Pride and stubbornness are luxuries you cannot afford.

5. *Intelligence is not a dirty word*. Those who govern a country should be the best and the brightest of the land. As Cicero says, if leaders don't have a thorough knowledge of what they are talking about, their speeches will be a silly prattle of empty words and their actions will be dangerously misguided.

6. *Compromise is the key to getting things done*. Cicero writes that in politics it is irresponsible to take an unwavering stand when circumstances are always evolving. There are times to

stand one's ground, but consistently refusing to yield is a sign of weakness, not strength.

7. *Don't raise taxes—unless you absolutely have to*. Every country needs revenue in order to function, but Cicero declares that a primary purpose of a government is to assure that individuals keep what belongs to them, not to redistribute wealth. On the other hand, he condemns the concentration of such wealth into the hands of the few and asserts that it is the duty of a country to provide fundamental services and security to its citizens.

8. *Immigration makes a country stronger*. Rome grew from a small village to a mighty empire by welcoming new citizens into its ranks as it spread across the Mediterranean. Even former slaves could become full voting members of society. New citizens bring new energy and ideas to a country.

9. *Never start an unjust war*. Of course the Romans, just like modern nations, believed they could justify any war they wanted to wage, but Cicero at least holds up the ideal that wars begun from greed rather than defense or to protect a country's honor are inexcusable.

10. *Corruption destroys a nation*. Greed, bribery, and fraud devour a country from the inside, leaving it weak and vulnerable. Corruption is not merely a moral evil, but a practical menace that leaves citizens at best disheartened, at worst seething with anger and ripe for revolution.

Even those who disagreed with Cicero couldn't help but admire the man. In his later years, Octavian, now the emperor Augustus, came upon his own grandson reading one of Cicero's works. The boy was terrified to be caught with a book written by a man his grandfather had condemned to death and so tried to hide it beneath his cloak. But Augustus took the book and read a long part of it while his frightened grandson watched. Then the old man handed it back to the youth saying, "A wise man, my child, a wise man and a lover of his country."

HOW TO RUN A COUNTRY

Natural Law

In the surviving passages of his book On the State, *Cicero provides a systematic discussion of political theory, including a famous passage on the idea that divine law underlies the universe and is the foundation on which government should be built. Cicero follows the Greek philosopher Aristotle and earlier Stoic teachers in upholding the idea of natural law—an idea fundamental to the founders of the American Republic regardless of their religious beliefs.*

True law is a harmony of right reasoning and nature. It applies to everyone in all places and times, for it is unchanging and everlasting. It commands each of us to do our duty and forbids us from doing wrong. Its commands and prohibitions guide good and prudent people, but those who are wicked will listen to neither. It is not right to try to alter this law. We cannot repeal any part of it, much less do away with it altogether. No senate or assembly of the people can free us from its obligations. We do not need anyone to explain or interpret it for us.

There is no such thing as one true law at Rome and another at Athens. There is no change of such law over time. It applies to all people everywhere—past, present, and future. There is one divine master and ruler over all of us who is creator, judge, and enforcer of this law. Those who disobey him are fleeing from themselves and are rejecting their own humanity. Even if they escape human judgment for their wrongdoing, they will pay a terrible price in the end.

In his book On Laws, *Cicero invents a dialogue between himself, his brother, and his best friend, Atticus, to lay out his plans for an ideal government. In the following selection, Cicero discusses why government is necessary and how it should function in accord with natural law.*

You realize, of course, that the job of a leader is to govern and to issue commands that are just, advantageous to the country, and in keeping with the law. The laws of a state rule over a leader just as he rules over the people. Indeed, we could say that a leader is the voice of the law and the law is a silent leader.

The rule of government should be in harmony with justice and the fundamental principles of nature, by which I mean it is in agreement with law. Without such government, no home or city or country nor indeed the human race, the natural world, or the universe itself could exist. For the universe obeys God just as the seas and lands obey the universe, so that all humanity is subject to this supreme law.

BALANCE OF POWER

To Cicero, the ideal government was one that combined the best qualities of a monarchy, an aristocracy, and a democracy—as was the case in the Roman Republic. The influence of his writings on the subject features prominently in the mixed constitution created by the American Founding Fathers.

Of the three main types of government, monarchy is in my opinion by far the most preferable. But a moderate and balanced form of government combining all three is even better than kingship. This sort of state would have an executive with preeminent and royal qualities, but also grant certain powers both to the leading citizens and to the people according to their wishes and judgment. This kind of constitution first of all offers a great degree of equality to citizens, something free people can scarcely do without for long, but it also provides stability. When one type of government alone rules, it frequently decays into the corresponding degenerate form—the king becomes a tyrant, the aristocracy turns into a factional oligarchy, and democracy becomes mob rule and anarchy. But while a single form of government often turns into something else, a mixed and balanced system remains stable, unless the leaders are unusually wicked. For there is no reason for a government to change when each citizen is guaranteed his own role and there is no underlying debased form into which it might slip and fall.

LEADERSHIP

Marcus Cicero loved to give advice, especially to his relatives and particularly to his younger brother Quintus. When Quintus was appointed governor of the important Roman province of Asia (on the western coast of modern Turkey) in 61 BC, Marcus couldn't resist sending him not one but two lengthy letters telling him how to do his job. Quintus was a perfectly capable administrator who would later serve bravely in Gaul under Julius Caesar, but he did have something of a temper and was prone to fits of melancholy. Although Quintus may not have welcomed the unsolicited advice from his brother, the first letter contains wise counsel for anyone facing the trials of public office.

So then, what I ask of you most of all is that you don't give in to despair or become discouraged. Don't allow yourself to be overwhelmed by a great flood of responsibilities. Rise up and face the difficulties that come your way or even go out to meet them. Fortune does not rule over your leadership in government. For the most part, your success depends on your own intelligence and hard work.

If you were thrown into some great, dangerous war and your term of office were extended, I might worry more that the winds of fortune could blow you about. But as I said, chance has nothing or at least very little to do with how you carry out your duties to your country. It depends much more on your own courage and thoughtful moderation. I don't think you need to worry about an ambush by enemies, fierce battles, being abandoned by our allies, running out of money or food for the troops, or that the army is going to mutiny against you. Such things do happen occasionally even to the wisest men, who are no more able to overcome misfortune than the best helmsmen can master a violent storm. Your job is to steer the ship of state smoothly and steadily. Remember that a helmsman who falls asleep can wreck a craft. Still, if you stay awake, you might enjoy the voyage.

Five years after Cicero's consulship in 63 BC, he was exiled from Italy by his political enemies on trumped-up charges. One of the few friends who stood by him was Publius Sestius, who was later unjustly charged by these same enemies with inciting public violence. Cicero defended him on his return to Rome and took the opportunity of the trial to outline his vision of a true leader and how citizens should respond when faced with threats to their freedom.

What destination should those steering the Republic keep their eyes fixed upon and by what course should they guide us there? The answer is what the most reasonable, decent, and blessed people always desire, namely peace with honor. Those who wish for this are our best citizens, those who make it happen are our best leaders and are considered the saviors of our country. These people who govern us should not be so carried away by their own political power that they turn away from peace, but neither should they embrace a peace that is dishonorable.

The founding principles of our Republic, the essence of peace with honor, the values that our leaders should defend and guard with their very lives if necessary are these: respecting religion, discovering the will of the gods, supporting the power of the magistrates, honoring the authority of the senate, obeying the law, valuing tradition, upholding the courts and their verdicts, practicing integrity, defending the provinces and our allies, and standing up for our country, our military, and our treasury.

Those who would be guardians of such important principles must be people of great courage, great ability, and great resolve. For among the crowds are those who would destroy our country through revolution and upheaval, either because they feel guilty about their own misdeeds and fear punishment, or because they are deranged enough to long for sedition and civil discord, or because of their own financial mismanagement they prefer to bring the whole country down in flames rather than burn alone. When such people find leaders to help them carry out their wicked plans, the Republic is tossed about on the waves. When this happens, those helmsmen who guide our country must be vigilant and use all their skill and diligence to preserve the principles I mentioned above and steer our country safely home with peace and honor.

Gentlemen of the jury, I don't deny that preserving the safety of our state is a steep, difficult, and dangerous path to tread. I would be lying if I said I haven't known and experienced the perils of this road more than most. The forces that attack our Republic are greater than those that defend her. Reckless and desperate men need only a small push to urge them to move against our country. But unfortunately, decent people are usually slow to act and ignore dangers until a crisis erupts. They are sluggish and willing to abide with peace without honor, but their own inaction causes them to lose both.

In his treatise On the State, *Cicero lays out his plans for an ideal government. Though the latter parts of the book are poorly preserved, the fragments that do survive present an inspiring vision of what a leader should be.*

The ideal state is one in which the best people desire praise and honor while avoiding humiliation and disgrace. Such citizens are not deterred from wrongdoing by a fear of punishment as laid out in the law as much as by an inborn sense of shame given to us by nature itself that makes us dread the thought of justified criticism. A true leader also encourages this natural feeling among others by using public opinion and enhances it through institutions and education so that shame encourages good citizenship no less than fear of legal penalties. . . .

Just as a helmsman desires a successful voyage or a doctor works for the health of a patient or a general plans for victory, so the leader of a country should strive for citizens to lead a happy life with financial security, abundant resources, good reputations, and honest virtue. This is what I yearn for from our leaders, for it should be their greatest and most noble goal.

Cicero began his political service to Rome in 75 BC as a quaestor supervising part of the province of Sicily and was posted to the town of Lilybaeum on the western coast of the island, far from the better-known Sicilian city of Syracuse. He performed his duties fairly and conscientiously, winning the praise of the Sicilians, who were accustomed to abusive officials intent only on looting the province for personal gain. Cicero was certain everyone in Rome must have been talking about the fine job he was doing and looked forward to basking in their praise when his term was finished. In a court speech from many years later, the older and wiser Cicero reflects on his experience as a young man returning to Italy as a much-needed lesson in humility.

Gentlemen of the jury, I hope you won't think I'm boasting if I speak of my experience as quaestor. It was certainly successful, but after all, I have served in many higher offices since then and don't need to seek glory from that time long ago. Still, I will say that no one ever had a more popular or praiseworthy term of service. By Hercules, I believed back then that all of Rome must have been talking about nothing except the marvelous job I was doing in Sicily. I managed to ship large amounts of grain to Rome in the middle of a critical food shortage. I was courteous to all the business-men, fair to the merchants, generous to the tax collectors, and honest in my dealings with the natives. Everyone there thought I had done a wonderful job handling my duties, and the Sicilians honored me like no previous quaestor. I departed the province hoping and believing that the people of Rome would fall all over themselves in praising me.

I left Sicily to make the journey back to Rome during the summer, and by chance I stopped at the resort of Puteoli, where many of the best Romans were vacationing at the time. I was thunderstruck, gentlemen, when someone I met there asked me on what day I had left Rome and if there was any news from the city. I answered him rather curtly that I was making my way back from a year abroad in my province.

"Oh yes, by Hercules," he said, "from Africa, I believe."

I was greatly annoyed and answered him disdainfully:

"No, I've just arrived from Sicily."

Then some know-it-all standing nearby butted in:

"What? Don't you know the fellow has been a quaestor in Syracuse?"

Why should I say more? At this point, I gave up and joined the crowd on the beach.

FRIENDS AND ENEMIES

Cicero made many friends and even more enemies as he climbed the political ladder. He worked tirelessly throughout his career to strengthen the state, especially in his exposure of a plot by the ruined nobleman Catiline to overthrow the elected government. One of his allies in this struggle was Metellus Celer, who raised an army in northern Italy to fight against Catiline and his band of disgruntled veterans. But the brother of Metellus was notably hostile to Cicero, putting him in the difficult position in the family-centered world of ancient Rome of working against a close relative of a friend. Metellus wrote a scathing letter to Cicero expressing his indignity at an attack on his brother, to which Cicero responds. The following selection reveals the letter as a model of how to handle an offended ally by addressing a problem directly and graciously explaining why it is sometimes necessary for a leader to stand up to a friend, even if there are political consequences.

From Marcus Tullius Cicero, son of Marcus, to Quintus Metellus Celer, son of Quintus, Proconsul.

I hope all is well with you and the army.

You wrote to me that because of our friendship and the restoration of good relations between us you never expected me to ridicule you. I'm not really sure what you mean by that, but I think that someone may have reported to you what I said in the senate. I declared there that there were many who were resentful that I had saved the Republic. I mentioned that a relative of yours, to whom you could not say no, had convinced you to suppress what you wanted to say in my favor on the senate floor. I also added that you and I had divided the duties of saving the country, so that I would protect Rome from domestic treachery and traitors within the city walls while you guarded the rest of Italy from armed enemies and hidden conspiracies. I continued that our partnership in so glorious and noble a task had been undermined by a member of your family who was afraid you might honor me by some gesture of mutual goodwill since I had so often praised you in warm and glowing terms. . . .

Let me assure you I did not attack your brother, but simply responded to his attack on me. My respect for you has not, as you wrote, wavered at all but has remained constant, even when you distanced yourself from me. Even now after you have written such a scathing letter to me, I can reply that not only do I forgive your harsh words but I commend you for your anger. I too have a brother whom I love, and my feelings for him guide me in this matter. I ask you likewise to understand my feelings. You must realize that when your brother attacked me harshly with such bitterness and without cause, I could not simply surrender to him. On the contrary, in such a situation I had every right to expect support from both you and your army.

I have always desired to be your friend and have tried to make you understand that our relationship means the world to me. My warm feelings for you have not changed and will not change, as long as you wish. Because of my affection for you, I would much rather abandon my quarrel with your brother than allow my disagreement with him to damage our friendship.

In contrast to the previous letter, the following passage, written only a year later, reveals a much more candid Cicero as he tells his friend Atticus about the current political situation in Rome. Atticus spent most of his adult life in Greece assiduously avoiding politics, though he maintained a great interest in Roman affairs and was always anxious for news.

Oh Atticus, since you left so much has happened that I should write about, but I haven't been able to risk a letter getting lost or being intercepted and opened. You should know they didn't let me speak first at the senate meeting but instead chose Piso, who brought such peace (hah!) to the land of the Allobroges in Gaul. The rest of the chamber murmured at this insult to me, but I didn't really care. At least now I don't have to be kind to that dreadful fellow and am free to maintain my stand against his political agenda. In any case, being second in line to speak is almost as prestigious as going first, and it saves me from feeling obligated to the consul in charge. Catullus spoke third, and, if you are still keeping track, Hortensius was fourth.

Our consul is an idiot with a perverse mind. He has a peevish way about him that makes people laugh even though he has no wit. His face is definitely funnier than his jokes. But at least he doesn't try to get involved in political decisions and has little to do with the conservative faction. He has neither the will to be useful to the country nor the courage to cause any real harm. His fellow consul, however, treats me with great respect and is an ardent defender of the conservative cause.

There is only a small disagreement between the consuls at present, though I'm afraid it may spread like a disease. I suppose you've heard how at the women's festival of the Good Goddess held at Caesar's house a man snuck in dressed in female clothing. The Vestal Virgins had to repeat the whole sacrifice. Later Quintus Cornificius (he wasn't one of our group, in case you were wondering) brought the issue before the senate.

It was referred back to the Vestals and the pontiffs, who formally pronounced the whole affair a sacrilege. Then the consuls and the senate brought forward a bill agreeing with the verdict, after which Caesar divorced his wife. Since Piso is a great friend of Clodius, he's working behind the scenes to defeat the bill that he himself proposed as a solemn senatorial decree on religion. Messalla is taking a hard line on the case. Clodius is persuading all the respectable people not to get involved in the matter. Gangs of thugs are being formed. I was as tough-minded as old Lycurgus at the start but am losing interest. Cato keeps on harping about it, as is his way. But enough about all that. Still, I am afraid that the indifference to the matter by good men and the attention paid to it by troublemakers may yet bode ill for the Republic.

That friend of yours—you know who I mean, the one you said started to praise me only when he no longer dared to criticize me—well, he acts like he's my best friend now. He hugs me, declares his warm feelings toward me, and openly praises me, but hides his jealousy just beneath his skin. He has no grace, no sincerity, no political savvy, no honesty, no courage, and no generosity—but I'll go into all that some other time.

PERSUASION

It's difficult for us today to imagine the importance of oratory in the ancient world. In an age before printing or electronic media, the ability of a leader to speak persuasively to crowds large and small was essential. But when Cicero talks about an orator, he means much more than someone who gives speeches. To him an orator was above all a statesman who was able to express the power of an idea to the public based on knowledge and wisdom. True Roman orators could persuade their audience to agree with them not because of verbal techniques, important as they might be, but because they knew what they were talking about and cared deeply for their country.

Indeed oratory involves much more than people realize and depends on a wide range of skills and abilities. The fact that so few are good at it is not due to a shortage of eager learners or teachers or even a lack of natural talent. There are an infinite variety of interesting cases available, and the rewards of success can be splendid. Why then are there so few who succeed? Because an orator must master an enormous number of difficult subjects.

If a person has not acquired a deep knowledge of all the necessary disciplines involved in oratory, his speech will be an endless prattle of empty and silly words. An orator must be able to choose the right language and arrange his words carefully. He must also understand the full range of emotions that nature has given us, for the ability to rouse or calm a crowd is the greatest test of both the understanding and the practical ability of a speaker. An orator also needs a certain charm and wit, the cultured ways of a gentleman, and the ability to strike fiercely when attacking an opponent. In addition he needs a subtle grace and sophistication. Finally, an orator must have a keen mind capable of remembering a vast array of relevant precedents and examples from history, along with a thorough knowledge of the law and civil statutes.

I'm sure I don't need to say much about the actual delivery of a speech. This includes the way in which an orator carries himself, how he uses gestures, the expressions on his face, the use of his voice, and making sure he is not monotonous. Pay special attention to that last one. You can see how important it is by looking at less serious art, by which I mean acting. For even though actors work very hard on their expressions, voices, and movements, there are precious few I would want to watch for long.

What shall I say about memory, that treasure house of all we know? Our minds hold all the words and ideas we use when thinking and speaking. Without a sharp memory, even the most carefully planned speech will be worthless.

So you can see why true orators are a rare breed. They must command a wide range of skills, though mastering even one of them would be considered quite an achievement. So let us urge our sons and anyone else whose reputation and glory matter to us to appreciate the magnitude and complexity of this task. They must not suppose they can become fine orators simply by following rules or finding a good teacher or going through some common exercises. They might have the ability to achieve their goal, but they must do much more.

I believe that no one can become a truly great orator unless he has a solid foundation in the whole range of human knowledge. This knowledge will ground and enrich everything he has to say. If an orator doesn't have this kind of background and learning, all he says will be vain and childish. Of course I'm not saying that an orator has to know everything, especially amid the hustle and bustle of modern life, but I am convinced that anyone who calls himself an orator must be able to competently handle any subject that comes his way, so that both the form and substance of his speeches will be of high quality. . . .

What could be more pleasing to the ear and to the mind than a beautiful speech adorned with wise thoughts and words carefully chosen? Think of the amazing power a single orator has to move an audience, to sway the verdict of jurors, or to shape the opinion of the senate. What could be more noble, more generous, more beautiful? An orator has the power to rescue supplicants, to lift the downtrodden, to bring deliverance to those in need, to free the oppressed from danger, and to stand up for the rights of citizens. . . .

I declare that the highest achievement of oratory is that it alone was able to bring together scattered people into one place, to start a wild and intemperate race on the road to human civilization, to establish communities, and to furnish them with laws that guarantee rights and justice. I could go on forever, but instead I will simply say that when a wise and moderate orator speaks well, he brings not only honor to himself, but also salvation to his fellow citizens and indeed to his whole country.

COMPROMISE

For Cicero, politics was the art of the possible, not a battleground of absolutes. He firmly believed in traditional values and the supremacy of law, but he also knew that in order to get things done the different factions in a country must be willing to work together.

When a small group of people control a nation because of their wealth or birth or some other advantage, they are simply a faction, even if they are called an aristocracy. On the other hand, if the multitude gains power and runs a country according to its wishes at the moment, it is called freedom, though it is in fact chaos. But when there is a tension between the common people and the aristocracy, with each man and group fearing the other, then neither can dominate, and an accommodation must be reached between the people and the powerful.

When Caesar, Pompey, and Crassus formed a triumvirate to rule Rome behind the scenes, they invited Cicero to join them. His principle prevented him from participation, though he was realistic enough to know that he had to work with the three men if he wanted to restore the Republic. In a later letter to his old friend Lentulus Spinther, he explains that a politician must sometimes swallow his pride for the greater good.

If I had seen the state ruled by the kind of villains and scoundrels who ran things during Cinna's time or at other nefarious periods of our history, no rewards could have enticed me to side with them (rewards mean little to me, no matter how much they might benefit me personally), nor could any threats (though I must admit that even the best of us can be moved by fear of personal danger). But the most powerful man in Rome was Pompey, who had earned all the glory and honor heaped on him by the greatest service to the state and by his military victories. I had supported him since I was a young man and also when I served as praetor and consul. He in turn supported me with his advice and voice in the senate, just as you did, helping me to achieve my own goals. I also had the same enemy in Rome as he did. Considering all this, I wasn't afraid of getting a reputation of inconsistency if now and then in certain speeches I urged others to support him, as he was such a great man and personal benefactor. . . .

So now you know my reasons for defending their cases and causes and why I conducted politics the way I did. I want to be clear that I would have done exactly the same things if I hadn't felt pressure from them. I wasn't foolish enough to fight such a formidable alliance nor would I want to deny the right of influential citizens to exercise power, even if it were possible for me to do so. In politics it is irresponsible to take an unwavering stand when circumstances are always evolving and good men change their minds. Clinging to the same opinion no matter the cost has never been considered a virtue among statesmen. When at sea, it is best to run before a storm if your ship can't make it to harbor. But if you can find safety by tacking back and forth, only a fool would hold a straight course rather than change directions and reach home. In the same way, a wise statesman should make peace with honor for his country the ultimate goal, as I have often said. It is our vision that must remain constant, not our words.

A year later, Crassus was dead in a battle with the Parthians, and soon Pompey and Caesar were preparing for civil war. The time had come for Cicero to choose sides. In spite of his internal deliberations voiced in the following letter to his friend Atticus, there was no doubt in his mind that compromise must at last be set aside for the good of the Republic.

Now, by Hercules, I ask you to favor me with your abundant wisdom in all things and to put all the love you feel for me into this single problem—help me decide what I must do! There is a great battle looming, perhaps the greatest history has ever known, unless the same god who unexpectedly delivered us in the war with the Parthians takes pity on the

Republic. There is no escape from this coming conflict, and so I will face it with everyone else. I don't ask you to consider that, but I implore you to help me with my particular situation. Don't you see that it's because of you I am close to both Pompey and Caesar? I wish I had listened to your kind words from the start, but, as Homer says, you could not sway the heart within my breast. At last you did persuade me to make peace with Pompey because of all he had done for me and with Caesar because of his power. Oh, how I worked to bring the two of them together and so won the affection of both, at least as much as any man could have. We calculated that if I were friends with Pompey I wouldn't have to set aside my political beliefs and that, since he was a close ally of Caesar, I ought to work with the latter as well. Now you and I can both see that the great battle between them is about to begin. Each of them counts me as his friend, unless one of them is only pretending, but I don't think Pompey doubts my loyalty, since I genuinely approve of his politics more than Caesar's. On the other hand, I just now received letters from both of them that arrived at the same time as yours assuring me that neither has anyone in the world they value more than me.

So what should I do? . . . There's no room left to sit on the fence.

Money and Power

Ancient Rome was a empire of haves and have-nots, with little in the way of a social safety net. Taxes could be onerous, but were needed to fund the large army. Since the second century BC, there had been proposals to reduce the tax burden and redistribute land and goods among veterans and the urban poor. Cicero did not object to easing the burden on the needy, but warns in his essay On Duties *against the dangers of politicians taking such sentiments too far. He also roundly condemns the greedy nature of those who serve in government only to serve themselves.*

In protecting the rights of individuals, we must always make sure what we're doing will also be beneficial, or at least not harmful, to our country. Gaius Gracchus began a massive distribution of grain to the people, but this exhausted the treasury. Marcus Octavius was more modest in handing out food to the poor, which was both manageable to the state and helpful to those in need. Thus he served the interests of both.

Whoever governs a country must first see to it that citizens keep what belongs to them and that the state does not take from individuals what is rightfully theirs. When Philippus was a tribune, he proposed a ruinous law to distribute land, though when his bill was voted down he took it very well and accepted defeat graciously. However, when he was defending the bill he pandered shamelessly to the common people, saying that there weren't more than two thousand people left in the city who owned any property. That kind of hyperbole must be condemned, along with any proposals advocating an equal distribution of goods. Can you imagine a more destructive agenda? Indeed, the chief reason we have a constitution and government at all is to protect individual property. Even though nature led people to come together into communities in the first place, they did so with the hope that they could keep what rightfully belonged to them.

Political leaders must try to avoid imposing a property tax as our ancestors did because of their empty treasury and constant wars. Precautions to prevent this kind of tax should be made far in advance. If it is absolutely necessary for a country to impose such a burden (I am not referring to Rome in particular, but indeed any nation), government leaders must make everyone realize that their safety and security depend on implementing such a tax.

It is also the job of those running a country to make sure citizens have an abundance of the necessities of life. I don't need to go into the details of what these are, for it should be obvious. It is enough that I mention it.

The most important thing for public officials to avoid is even the suspicion of greed and personal gain. Long ago, Gaius Pontius the Samnite said, "I wish fate had allowed me to live in an age when Romans accepted bribes. Then I wouldn't have to put up with their rule!" He would have waited many generations for this to happen, for only recently has the evil of corruption reached our country. I'm glad therefore that Pontius lived when he did, for he was a mighty man. It's been only a little over a century since Lucius Piso passed a bill to punish extortion. Before that, there was no need for such a law. There have been many similar laws since then, each more harsh than the last, and many officials brought up on charges and convicted. The war with our Italian allies was caused because of Roman fear of conviction on such charges. When the laws and courts were overturned, our allies suffered great plundering and pillaging. We seem to be powerful nowadays only because of the weakness of others, not because of our own strength.

Panaetius praises Africanus for his integrity. Well, why shouldn't he? Though there were greater qualities he possessed. Indeed, when you praise the integrity of a man you are also praising the age in which he lived. When Paullus conquered the Macedonians and brought back all their enormous wealth, he carried into our treasury so much money that the spoils won by a single general did away with the need for all property taxes. The only thing he kept for himself was the undying glory of his name. Africanus imitated his father and profited not at all from his conquest of Carthage. And remember his colleague in the censorship, Lucius Mummius? Was he a penny richer when he destroyed Corinth, that wealthiest of cities? He preferred to adorn Italy, not his own house, though it seems to me by benefiting Italy he adorned his own house all the more.

But I digress from the point of our discussion, which is that there is no greater vice than greed, especially among those governing our country. For to use public office for personal gain is not only immoral, but also criminal and just plain wicked. When the oracle of Apollo at Delphi told the Spartans that the only enemy who could conquer them was greed, she wasn't speaking just to them but to every prosperous nation. For those politicians who wish to gain the favor of the public, there is no better way than self-restraint and honesty.

As for those politicians who pretend they are friends of the common people and try to pass laws redistributing property and drive people out of their homes or champion legislation forgiving loans, I say they are undermining the very foundations of our state. They are destroying social harmony, which cannot exist when you take away money from some to give it to others. They are also destroying fairness, which vanishes when people cannot keep what rightfully belongs to them. For as I have said, it is the proper role of the government to guard the right of citizens to control their own property.

Cicero believed strongly in private property rights, but also he saw great danger when a limited number of people controlled the financial resources of a country.

For years, we have watched in silence while all the wealth of the world is gathered into the hands of a few men. Our willingness to let this happen is all the more evident because none of these men even bothers to pretend he is not doing wrong or tries to conceal his greed.

IMMIGRATION

In 56 BC, the conservatives in the senate realized they could not attack Julius Caesar directly while he was leading a successful war in Gaul, so they staged a proxy fight against one of his closest aides, a wealthy foreigner named Balbus from the city of Gades on the Atlantic coast of the Iberian peninsula. Balbus had received Roman citizenship over fifteen years earlier from Pompey for his service to Rome. Cicero felt compelled by his alliance at the time with Caesar and Pompey to defend Balbus, but his arguments go beyond the particular occasion of the trial to illustrate the Roman attitude toward extending citizenship to outsiders. Unlike many Greek cities, the Romans welcomed worthy foreigners (such as the Apostle Paul) and even former slaves as full citizens. Cicero's ancestors at the Volscian hilltown of Arpinum had benefited from such a grant of citizenship in the previous century, and so we may imagine he was sympathetic to the cause. Cicero believed that a nation that welcomes outsiders into its ranks as equal members becomes stronger, not weaker.

If our generals, if the senate, if the Roman people themselves will not be permitted to offer the reward of citizenship to the best and bravest of our allies and friends who risk their lives for our safety and security, then we are going to find ourselves sorely lacking in valuable help in difficult and dangerous times. . . .

We know that Roman citizenship has been granted to tax-paying communities in Africa, Sicily, Sardinia, and in many other provinces. We also know that enemies who have surrendered to our generals and provided valuable services to the Republic have been given citizenship. And of course even slaves, whose legal standing is as low as it can be, have been given their freedom and thus Roman citizenship because they have served our country well. . . .

I want to make clear the crucial principle that a citizen of any nation on this earth—whether that country is estranged from the Roman people because of hatred and hostility or greatly beloved and bound to us because of their faithful service—can be welcomed into our nation and given the gift of Roman citizenship. . . .

Without a doubt what has done the most to increase the power and reputation of the Roman people is the precedent laid down by Romulus, the founder of our city, when he made a treaty with the Sabines and showed us that we make ourselves stronger by welcoming even our enemies as citizens. Our ancestors never forgot his example in granting and bestowing citizenship on others.

WAR

The Greeks and Romans had no illusions about war. From Homer's Iliad *to Caesar's* Gallic War, *the horrors and terrible human cost are plain to see. But neither did they shrink from war when they felt is was necessary. Waging war to protect one's country, support allies, or maintain honor was considered perfectly acceptable by all. Cicero agrees with this philosophy and argues in one of his earliest political speeches that protecting the honor of a country can be the most compelling reason to go to war. The occasion was the proposal to allow his patron Pompey to take up a military command against Mithradates, a long-standing nemesis of Rome who ruled in Asia Minor.*

Our ancestors often went to war for the sake of modest insults against our merchants or ship owners, so how do you feel when with a single word Mithradates ordered the slaughter of thousands of Roman citizens? Our forefathers utterly destroyed the city of Corinth, that shining light of Greece, because its citizens showed disrespect to our ambassadors. But you will allow this king to go unpunished after he put our ambassador, a former consul of the Roman people, in chains, then scourged and brutalized him in every possible way before killing him? Our ancestors would not have allowed Roman citizens to suffer mere mistreatment, but you stand idly by while they are murdered! They took vengeance when legates were merely insulted, while you, on the other hand, do nothing after our ambassador has been tortured to death. Beware lest this great country that our forefathers bestowed on you becomes your greatest shame—because you were not willing to defend it.

Cicero argues that some wars are justified whereas others are not. This doctrine of a just war is stated most clearly in the surviving fragments of his later work, On the State.

A good country does not begin a war except to defend its honor or to protect itself. . . .

Wars are unjust if they are undertaken without cause. Only a war waged in retaliation or defense can be considered just. . . .

No war is honorable unless it is announced and declared or it is for the recovery of property.

CORRUPTION

The abuse of power was rampant in the late Roman Republic, especially among those members of the nobility who were sent abroad to govern provinces. The privilege of these Roman wolves to feast on the provincial sheep was often protected by members of the senate, who had behaved similarly themselves or hoped to in the future. But honest men such as Cicero believed that corruption was a cancer that ate at the heart of a state. In the following passages, taken from one of Cicero's earliest speeches, Gaius Verres, a former governor of the island of Sicily now on trial, is held up as the epitome of the crooked politician out to profit from his term in office.

Gentlemen of the jury, I know that you are all quite aware that Gaius Verres shamelessly looted Sicily of all its goods, sacred and secular, public and private. You know as well as I do that he openly committed every kind of thievery and plunder without the slightest concern about morality or being caught. . . .

When spring began during his governorship—which by the way wasn't made known to him by a warm west wind or rising constellation, but rather the appearance of a fresh rose on his dinner table—that was when he began his toilsome rounds about the province. He displayed such vigor and endurance at the task that no one ever saw him riding a horse. No, like a king of Bithynia he was borne about on a litter carried by eight men. Inside was an elegant cushion stuffed with rose petals from Malta. Inside also was Verres, wearing two garlands, one on his head and the other about his neck. Close to his nose, he held a netted bag of the finest linen also stuffed with rose petals. That is how he made his official journeys about the island, carried straight into his bedroom wherever he was staying. To those same chambers came Sicilian officials and Roman businessmen, as many witnesses have told you. He decided legal disputes in private, announcing them only later in public. Thus he spent his time in bed issuing rulings, not caring at all about justice but concerned very much with making money.

But this onerous duty didn't take up his whole day, for he managed to squeeze Venus and Bacchus into his busy schedule. I must share with you the great diligence and care our brave commander devoted to such activities. In every town of Sicily where governors are accustomed to visit, some woman of a respectable family was chosen to satisfy his lust. Some of them were brought openly to his dinner table, while others were smuggled in under cover of darkness to avoid being seen by those gathered about.

These dinners of Verres were not the modest affairs you would expect from a Roman governor and general, nor did they conform to the decorum normally observed at the tables of Roman officials. They were filled with noise and shouting, often degenerating into fist fights. Our devoted governor never bothered much with rules and regulations in his job, but when it came to wine he was most conscientious and applied himself with gusto. It was a sight to see,

with guests carried away from his parties under people's arms like wounded men from the
battlefield. Others were left sprawling on the
floor like corpses, while the rest lay about like
drunken fools. Anyone wandering by would
have thought he wasn't looking at the dinner
party of a Roman governor but at a debauched
reenactment of the Battle of Cannae. . . .

Because of the corruption and greed of
Verres, the Roman fleet in Sicily was a navy
in name only. The ships were almost empty
of crews, and those that had men were better
suited to serving the avarice of the governor
than chasing away pirates. Still, when the cap-
tains Publius Cassius and Publius Tadius were
at sea with their ten undermanned ships, they
did happen upon one ship of brigands full of
treasure. They didn't so much capture it as
stumble upon it as it slowly made its way along
weighed down by plunder. The ship was full

of silver coins and plates, precious cloth—and handsome young men.

They found this single ship near Megara Hyblaea, not far from Syracuse. When Verres was told, he was lying down drunk surrounded by young women, but he found the strength to jump up right away and order his guards to go at once to his quaestor and legate and see that everything was brought to him untouched. The ship and crew were brought to Syracuse, where everyone expected justice to be done, but instead Verres acted as if everything belonged to him. Those pirates who were old or ugly he had put to death as enemies of the state. Those who were attractive or possessing some skill he took for himself, though he gave away a few to his secretaries, his assistants, and his son. Six of the captured men who were musicians he sent to a friend in Rome. It took them all night to unload the rest of the treasure from the ship. . . .

And so, gentlemen of the jury, I hope that I can finish this prosecution knowing that I have done my duty both to the Sicilians and to the Roman people. But I want everyone to know that if you do not live up to my high expectations and fail to convict Verres, I will continue my work and bring charges against anyone who might have offered you bribes as well as against anyone among you who might have brought guilt upon himself by accepting them. So let me say to those who would dare to play their cunning tricks and interfere with the pursuit of justice against the defendant in this case, beware, for they must be prepared to deal with me when I expose them to the Roman people. I hope they will see that I have been vehement, persevering, and vigilant as a prosecutor of this enemy of our Sicilian allies. Let them know that I will be just as adamant and relentless as a prosecutor in the future if the need arises and even more so, for I shall be speaking on behalf of the Roman people.

Tyranny

Cicero lived at a time when the ancient freedoms of the Roman Republic were disappearing. The rights of the people and their elected representatives were being replaced by men who used military force to gain power and enrich themselves. To Cicero, rule by a single leader, even one as capable as Julius Caesar, was an invitation to disaster, as absolute power inevitably corrupts even the best of men.

People submit themselves to the authority and power of another person for a variety of reasons. Sometimes they do it because of goodwill or gratitude for favor shown to them. Sometimes they do it because of the dignity of a person or because they hope to profit from the act. Some people subordinate themselves fearing that if they don't, the other person will make them submit anyway. Sometimes people surrender their freedom because of gifts or promises. Finally, as has so often been the case in our own country, people submit to the power of another because of outright bribes.

The best way for a man to gain authority over others and maintain it is through genuine affection. The worst way, however, is through fear. Wise Ennius once said: "People hate the man they fear—and whomever they hate, they want to see dead." Just recently we've learned, as if we didn't know it already, that no amount of power can stand up to the hatred of the people. The death of Caesar, who ruled the state through armed force (and whose legacy still rules us) shows better than anything the terrible price paid by all tyrants. You will have a difficult time finding any despot who doesn't end up like him. I say it again, using fear to maintain power simply doesn't work. But the leader who keeps the goodwill of his people is secure.

Those rulers who wish to keep their subjects under control by force will have to use brutal methods, just as a master must when dealing with rebellious slaves. Whoever tries to govern a country through fear is quite mad. For no matter how much a tyrant might try to overturn the law and crush the spirit of freedom, sooner or later it will rise up again either through public outrage or the ballot box. Freedom suppressed and risen again bites with sharper teeth than if it had never been lost. Therefore remember what is true always and everywhere and what is the strongest support of prosperity and power, namely that kindness is stronger than fear. That is the best rule for governing a country and for leading one's own life.

Cicero hated tyranny of all kinds, whether it was rule by one man, a small group, or an unruly mob. In an imaginary dialogue set in the past between the great Roman general Scipio and his friend Laelius, he condemns all three.

SCIPIO: How can a state ruled by a tyrant be called a republic at all? For that is what *republic* means—*res publica*, "the property of the people." No country where everyone is oppressed by a single man, where there is no common bond of justice, where there is no agreement among those coming together, can ever belong to the people. Take Syracuse, that most glorious of cities, which Timaeus calls the greatest Greek town and more beautiful than any other. Its citadel was a sight to behold, as were its port and harbor, whose waters reached to the heart of the city and the foundations of its buildings. Its streets were broad with magnificent colonnades, temples, and walls. Yet it certainly could not be called a republic while Dionysius ruled, because everything belonged to him. Therefore, wherever a tyrant rules we ought not to say that it is a bad republic—as I know I said yesterday—because it really isn't a republic at all.

LAELIUS: Well said, Scipio. Now I understand what you were talking about earlier.

SCIPIO: So you see that even a country controlled by a small number of men rather than a dictator cannot be called a republic?

LAELIUS: Yes, I certainly do.

SCIPIO: And you would be right to believe so. Where was the "property of the people" when after the great Peloponnesian War the notorious Thirty took over Athens? Did the ancient glory of that state or its splendid buildings, theaters, gymnasiums, colonnades, noble Propylaea, acropolis, works of art by Phidias, or magnificent port of Piraeus make it a republic?

LAELIUS: No, of course not, since nothing truly belonged to the people.

SCIPIO: What about when the Board of Ten ruled in Rome without any right of appeal, when freedom had lost all its defenses?

LAELIUS: There was no such thing then as a republic. Indeed, the people soon rose up to regain their liberty.

SCIPIO: Consider now a third type of government that can also cause many problems, namely democracy. Suppose in such a state the people control everything and all power is in their hands. The masses inflict punishment on whomever they choose and seize, plunder, keep, or distribute whatever they want. Isn't that the very definition, Laelius, of a state in which the property belongs to the people? Wouldn't you describe that as the perfect republic?

LAELIUS: I certainly would not! There is no state less deserving of the name than one in which all property is subject to the whims of the multitude. We have already decided that no republic existed in Syracuse or Agrigentum or Athens when they were ruled by tyrants nor here in Rome when the Board of Ten was in charge. I cannot see how despotism is lessened when a state is ruled by a mob. As you wisely said, Scipio, a true republic can exist only when the citizens consent to be bound together under the law. The monstrosity you describe surely deserves the name of tyranny just as much as if it were a single person. Actually, it is even worse, for there is nothing more despicable than a government that falsely assumes the appearance and name of "the people."

After the Ides of March in 44 BC and the murder of Julius Caesar, Cicero and his companions hoped freedom might be reborn in Rome. But the death of Caesar only set the stage for the rise of new tyrants and the end of the Republic. When Mark Antony and Octavian took up the reins of power, Cicero believed Octavian (the future emperor Augustus) might yet restore the ancient traditions, but he harbored no such illusions about Antony. In a series of speeches, he repeatedly condemned Antony as a tyrant. Cicero would pay for his boldness with his life.

I will compare you, Antony, to Caesar in your lust for power, but in nothing else. For although that man inflicted many evils on the

Republic, the one thing I will say for him is that he taught the Roman people how much faith they could place in someone, to whom they could entrust themselves, and what kind of person they should guard against. Haven't you considered this? Don't you understand that brave men have learned how beautiful, how rewarding, how glorious it is to slay a tyrant? Do you really think that when they did not endure him, they will endure you? Believe me, from now on men will not wait around for some convenient opportunity to present itself to do the deed.

Please, come to your senses. Consider those from whom you are descended, not those among whom you live now. Treat me as you will, but don't turn your back on the Republic. Nevertheless, in the end you must decide which path you will follow, as I have. I defended my country when I was young; I will not desert it as an old man. I despised the sword of Catiline; I will not be afraid of yours.

I would gladly lay down my life if my death might restore freedom to my country, so that the pain of the Roman people might give way at last to a new birth. Almost twenty years ago, I declared in this very temple that a man who had reached the office of consul should not fear death. How much more this is true now in my old age. Truly, my fellow senators, I would welcome death now that the honors I earned and deeds I performed are in the past. I only wish for two things: first, that my death might restore liberty to the Roman people—the gods could grant me no greater gift—and second, that each man will get his just reward depending on how he served his country.

Cicero's Epilogue: The Fallen State

The Roman state is founded firm on ancient
customs and its men.

—Ennius, *Annales*

The poet who wrote these words so brief and
true seems to me to have heard them from a
divine oracle. For neither men by themselves
without a state based on strong customs nor
traditions without men to defend them could
have established and maintained a republic
such as ours whose power stretches so far and
wide. Before our time, the cherished customs
of our forefathers produced exceptional and
admirable men who preserved the ways and
institutions of our ancestors.

But now our republic looks like a beautiful painting faded with age. Our generation
has not only failed to restore the colors of this

masterpiece, but we have not even bothered to preserve its general form and outline. What now remains of the ancient ways of our country the poet declares we were founded upon? These traditions have so sunk into oblivion that we neither practice them nor even remember what they were. And what shall I say about the men? For the reason our customs have passed away is that the people who once upheld them no longer exist. We should be put on trial as if for a capital crime to explain why this disaster has happened. But there is no defense we can give. Our country survives only in words, not as anything of substance. We have lost it all. We have only ourselves to blame.

LATIN TEXTS

NATURAL LAW

On the State 3.33: Est quidem vera lex recta ratio naturae congruens, diffusa in omnes, constans, sempiterna, quae vocet ad officium iubendo, vetando a fraude deterreat; quae tamen neque probos frustra iubet aut vetat nec improbos iubendo aut vetando movet. Huic legi nec obrogari fas est neque derogari ex hac aliquid licet neque tota abrogari potest. Nec vero aut per senatum aut per populum solvi hac lege possumus, neque est quaerendus explanator aut interpres eius alius; nec erit alia lex Romae, alia Athenis, alia nunc, alia posthac, sed et omnes gentes et omni tempore una lex et

sempiterna et immutabilis continebit, unusque
erit communis quasi magister et imperator
omnium deus, ille legis huius inventor, discep-
tator, lator, cui qui non parebit ipse se fugiet,
ac naturam hominis aspernatus hoc ipso luet
maximas poenas, etiamsi cetera supplicia, quae
putantur, effugerit.

On Laws 3.2–3: Videtis igitur magistratus
hanc esse vim, ut praesit praescribatque recta
et utilia et coniuncta cum legibus. Vt enim
magistratibus leges, sic populo praesunt
magistratus vereque dici potest, magistratum
legem esse loquentem, legem autem mutum
magistratum. Nihil porro tam aptum est ad
ius condicionemque naturae (quod cum dico,
legem a me dici intellegi volo) quam imperium,
sine quo nec domus ulla nec civitas nec gens
nec hominum universum genus stare, nec
rerum natura omnis nec ipse mundus potest;

nam et hic deo paret, et huic oboediunt maria terraeque, et hominum vita iussis supremae legis obtemperat.

BALANCE OF POWER

On the State 1.69: Ex tribus primis generibus longe praestat mea sententia regium; regio autem ipsi praestabit id quod erit aequatum et temperatum ex tribus optimis rerum publicarum modis. Placet enim esse quiddam in re publica praestans et regale, esse aliud auctoritati principum inpartitum ac tributum, esse quasdam res servatas iudicio voluntatique multitudinis. Haec constitutio primum habet aequabilitatem quandam magnam, qua carere diutius vix possunt liberi, deinde firmitudinem, quod et illa prima facile in contraria vitia convertuntur, ut existat ex rege dominus, ex optimatibus factio, ex populo turba et confusio, quodque ipsa genera generibus saepe conmutantur novis, hoc in hac iuncta moderateque permixta conformatione rei publicae non ferme sine magnis principum vitiis evenit. Non est enim causa conversionis, ubi in suo quisque est gradu firmiter collocatus et non subest, quo praecipitet ac decidat.

LEADERSHIP

Letter to Quintus 1.1.4–5: Quapropter hoc te primum rogo ne contrahas ac demittas animum neve te obrui tamquam fluctu sic magnitudine negoti sinas contraque erigas ac resistas sive etiam ultro occurras negotiis. Neque enim eius modi partem rei publicae geris in qua fortuna dominetur, sed in qua plurimum ratio possit et diligentia. Quod si tibi bellum aliquod magnum et periculosum administranti prorogatum imperium viderem, tremerem animo quod eodem tempore esse intellegerem etiam fortunae potestatem in nos prorogatam. Nunc vero ea pars tibi rei publicae commissa est in qua aut nullam aut perexiguam partem fortuna tenet et quae mihi tota in tua virtute ac moderatione animi posita esse videatur. Nullas, ut opinor, insidias hostium, nullam proeli dimicationem, nullam defectionem sociorum, nullam inopiam stipendi aut rei frumentariae, nullam seditionem exercitus pertimescimus, quae persaepe sapientissimis viris acciderunt, ut, quem ad modum gubernatores optimi vim tempestatis, sic illi fortunae impetum superare non possent. Tibi data est summa pax, summa tranquillitas, ita tamen ut ea dormientem gubernatorem vel obruere, vigilantem etiam delectare possit.

In Defense of Sestius 98–100: Quid est igitur propositum his rei publicae gubernatoribus quod intueri et quo cursum suum derigere debeant? Id quod est praestantissimum maximeque optabile omnibus sanis et bonis et beatis, cum dignitate otium. Hoc qui volunt, omnes optimates, qui efficiunt, summi viri et conservatores civitatis putantur; neque enim rerum gerendarum dignitate homines ecferri ita convenit ut otio non prospiciant, neque ullum amplexari otium quod abhorreat a dignitate.

Huius autem otiosae dignitatis haec fundamenta sunt, haec membra, quae tuenda principibus et vel capitis periculo defendenda sunt: religiones, auspicia, potestates magistratuum, senatus auctoritas, leges, mos maiorum, iudicia, iuris dictio, fides, provinciae, socii, imperi laus, res militaris, aerarium. Harum rerum tot atque tantarum esse defensorem et patronum magni animi est, magni ingeni magnaeque constantiae. Etenim in tanto civium numero magna multitudo est eorum qui aut propter metum poenae, peccatorum suorum conscii, novos motus conversionesque rei publicae quaerant, aut qui propter insitum quendam animi furorem discordiis civium ac seditione pascantur, aut qui propter implicationem rei familiaris communi incendio malint quam suo deflagrare. Qui cum tutores sunt et duces suorum studiorum vitiorumque nacti, in re publica fluctus excitantur, ut vigilandum sit iis qui sibi gubernacula patriae depoposcerunt, enitendumque omni scientia ac diligentia ut, conservatis iis quae ego paulo ante fundamenta ac membra esse dixi, tenere cursum possint et capere oti illum portum et dignitatis. Hanc ego viam, iudices, si aut asperam atque arduam aut plenam esse periculorum aut insidiarum negem, mentiar, praesertim cum id non modo intellexerim semper, sed etiam praeter ceteros senserim.

Maioribus praesidiis et copiis oppugnatur res publica quam defenditur, propterea quod audaces homines et perditi nutu impelluntur et ipsi etiam sponte sua contra rem publicam incitantur, boni nescio quo modo tardiores sunt et principiis rerum neglectis ad extremum ipsa denique necessitate excitantur, ita ut non numquam cunctatione ac tarditate, dum otium volunt etiam sine dignitate retinere, ipsi utrumque amittant.

On the State 5.6, 8: Civitatibus in quibus expetunt laudem optumi et decus, ignominiam fugiunt ac dedecus. Nec vero tam metu poenaque terrentur, quae est constituta legibus, quam verecundia, quam natura homini dedit quasi quendam vituperationis non iniustae timorem. Hanc ille rector rerum publicarum auxit opinionibus perfecitque institutis et disciplinis, ut pudor civis non minus a delictis arceret quam metus. Atque haec quidem ad laudem pertinent, quae dici latius uberiusque potuerunt. . . .

Ut enim gubernatori cursus secundus, medico salus, imperatori victoria, sic huic moderatori rei publicae beata civium vita proposita est, ut opibus firma, copiis locuples, gloria ampla, virtute honesta sit. Huius enim operis maximi inter homines atque optimi illum esse perfectorem volo.

For Plancius 64–65: Non vereor ne mihi aliquid, iudices, videar adrogare, si de quaestura mea dixero. Quamvis enim illa floruerit, tamen eum me postea fuisse in maximis imperiis arbitror ut non ita multum mihi gloriae sit ex quaesturae laude repetendum. Sed tamen non vereor ne quis audeat dicere ullius in Sicilia quaesturam aut clariorem aut gratiorem fuisse. Vere me hercule hoc dicam: sic tum existimabam, nihil homines aliud Romae nisi de quaestura mea loqui. Frumenti in summa caritate maximum numerum

miseram; negotiatoribus comis, mercatoribus
iustus, mancipibus liberalis, sociis abstinens,
omnibus eram visus in omni officio diligentis-
simus; excogitati quidam erant a Siculis honores
in me inauditi. Itaque hac spe decedebam ut mihi
populum Romanum ultro omnia delaturum
putarem. At ego cum casu diebus eis itineris
faciendi causa decedens e provincia Puteolos
forte venissem, cum plurimi et lautissimi in eis
locis solent esse, concidi paene, iudices, cum ex
me quidam quaesisset quo die Roma exissem et
num quidnam esset novi. Cui cum respondissem
me e provincia decedere: "etiam me hercule,"
inquit, "ut opinor, ex Africa." Huic ego iam sto-
machans fastidiose: "immo ex Sicilia," inquam.
Tum quidam, quasi qui omnia sciret: "quid?
tu nescis," inquit, "huic quaestorem Syracusis
fuisse?" Quid multa? destiti stomachari et me
unum ex eis feci qui ad aquas venissent.

FRIENDS AND ENEMIES

Letter to Metellus Celer 5.2.1, 10: Si tu exercitusque valetis, benest. Scribis ad me "te existimasse pro mutuo inter nos animo et pro reconciliata gratia numquam te a me ludibrio laesum iri." Quod cuius modi sit, satis intellegere non possum, sed tamen suspicor ad te esse adlatum me in senatu, cum disputarem permultos esse qui rem publicam a me conservatam dolerent, dixisse a te propinquos tuos, quibus negare non potuisses, impetrasse ut ea, quae statuisses tibi in senatu de mea laude esse dicenda, reticeres. Quod cum dicerem, illud adiunxi, mihi tecum ita dispertitum officium fuisse in rei publicae salute retinenda, ut ego urbem a domesticis insidiis et ab intestino scelere, tu Italiam et ab armatis hostibus et ab occulta coniuratione defenderes, atque hanc nostram tanti et tam praeclari muneris societatem a tuis propinquis labefactatam, qui, cum tu a me rebus amplissimis atque honorificentissimis ornatus esses, timuissent ne quae mihi pars abs te voluntatis mutuae tribueretur. . . .

Quare non ego "oppugnavi" fratrem tuum, sed fratri tuo repugnavi nec in te, ut scribis, "animo fui mobili," sed ita stabili, ut in mea erga te voluntate etiam desertus ab officiis tuis permanerem. Atque hoc ipso tempore tibi paene minitanti nobis per litteras hoc rescribo atque respondeo: Ego dolori tuo non solum ignosco, sed summam etiam laudem tribuo (meus enim me sensus, quanta vis fraterni sit amoris, admonet); a te peto ut tu quoque aequum te iudicem dolori meo praebeas; si acerbe, si crudeliter, si sine causa sum a tuis oppugnatus, ut statuas mihi non modo non cedendum sed etiam tuo atque exercitus tui auxilio in eius modi causa utendum fuisse. Ego te mihi semper amicum esse volui, me ut tibi amicissimum esse intellegeres laboravi. Maneo in voluntate et, quoad voles tu, permanebo citiusque amore tui fratrem tuum odisse desinam quam illius odio quicquam de nostra benevolentia detraham.

Letter to Atticus 1.13.2–4: Sunt autem post discessum a me tuum res dignae litteris nostris, sed non committendae eius modi periculo ut aut interire aut aperiri aut intercipi possint. Primum igitur scito primum me non esse rogatum sententiam praepositumque esse nobis pacificatorem Allobrogum, idque admurmurante senatu neque me invito esse factum. Sum enim et ab observando homine perverso liber et ad dignitatem in re publica retinendam contra illius voluntatem solutus, et ille secundus in dicendo locus habet auctoritatem paene principis et voluntatem non nimis devinctam beneficio consulis. Tertius est Catulus, quartus, si etiam hoc quaeris, Hortensius. Consul autem ipse parvo animo et pravo tamen cavillator genere illo moroso quod etiam sine dicacitate ridetur, facie magis quam facetiis ridiculus, nihil agens cum re publica, seiunctus ab optimatibus, a quo nihil speres boni rei publicae quia non vult, nihil speres mali quia non audet. Eius autem conlega et in me perhonorificus et partium studiosus ac defensor bonarum. Qui nunc leviter inter se dissident. Sed vereor ne hoc quod infectum est serpat longius. Credo enim te audisse, cum apud Caesarem pro populo fieret, venisse eo muliebri vestitu virum, idque sacrificium cum virgines instaurassent, mentionem a Q. Cornificio in senatu factam (is fuit princeps, ne tu forte aliquem nostrum putes); postea rem ex senatus consulto ad virgines atque ad pontifices relatam idque ab iis nefas esse decretum; deinde ex senatus consulto consules rogationem promulgasse; uxori Caesarem nuntium remisisse. In hac causa Piso amicitia P. Clodi ductus operam dat ut ea rogatio quam ipse fert et fert ex senatus consulto et de religione antiquetur. Messalla vehementer adhuc agit severe. Boni viri precibus Clodi removentur a causa, operae comparantur, nosmet ipsi, qui Lycurgei a principio fuissemus, cotidie demitigamur, instat et urget Cato. Quid multa? Vereor ne haec neglecta a bonis, defensa ab improbis magnorum rei publicae malorum causa sit.

Tuus autem ille amicus (scin quem dicam?), de quo tu ad me scripsisti, postea quam non auderet reprehendere, laudare coepisse, nos, ut ostendit, admodum diligit, amplectitur, amat, aperte laudat, occulte sed ita ut perspicuum sit invidet. Nihil come, nihil simplex, nihil ἐν τοῖς πολιτικοῖς inlustre, nihil honestum, nihil forte, nihil liberum. Sed haec ad te scribam alias subtilius.

Persuasion

On the Orator 1.16–21, 31, 33–34: Sed enim maius est hoc quiddam quam homines opinantur, et pluribus ex artibus studiisque conlectum. Quid enim quis aliud in maxima discentium multitudine, summa magistrorum copia, praestantissimis hominum ingeniis, infinita causarum varietate, amplissimis eloquentiae propositis praemiis esse causae putet, nisi rei quandam incredibilem magnitudinem ac difficultatem? Est enim et scientia comprehendenda rerum plurimarum, sine qua verborum volubilitas inanis atque inridenda est, et ipsa oratio conformanda non solum electione, sed etiam constructione verborum, et omnes animorum motus, quos hominum generi rerum natura tribuit, penitus pernoscendi, quod omnis vis ratioque dicendi in eorum, qui audiunt, mentibus aut sedandis

aut excitandis expromenda est; accedat eodem
oportet lepos quidam facetiaeque et eruditio
libero digna celeritasque et brevitas et respon-
dendi et lacessendi subtili venustate atque ur-
banitate coniuncta; tenenda praeterea est omnis
antiquitas exemplorumque vis, neque legum ac
iuris civilis scientia neglegenda est. Nam quid
ego de actione ipsa plura dicam? Quae motu
corporis, quae gestu, quae vultu, quae vocis
conformatione ac varietate moderanda est;
quae sola per se ipsa quanta sit, histrionum
levis ars et scaena declarat; in qua cum omnes
in oris et vocis et motus moderatione laborent,
quis ignorat quam pauci sint fuerintque, quos
animo aequo spectare possimus? Quid dicam
de thesauro rerum omnium, memoria? Quae
nisi custos inventis cogitatisque rebus et
verbis adhibeatur, intellegimus omnia, etiam
si praeclarissima fuerint in oratore, peritura.
Quam ob rem mirari desinamus, quae causa

sit eloquentium paucitatis, cum ex eis rebus universis eloquentia constet, in quibus singulis elaborare permagnum est, hortemurque potius liberos nostros ceterosque, quorum gloria nobis et dignitas cara est, ut animo rei magnitudinem complectantur neque eis aut praeceptis aut magistris aut exercitationibus, quibus utuntur omnes, sed aliis quibusdam se id quod expetunt, consequi posse confidant. Ac mea quidem sententia nemo poterit esse omni laude cumulatus orator, nisi erit omnium rerum magnarum atque artium scientiam consecutus: etenim ex rerum cognitione efflorescat et redundet oportet oratio. Quae, nisi res est ab oratore percepta et cognita, inanem quandam habet elocutionem et paene puerilem. Neque vero ego hoc tantum oneris imponam nostris praesertim oratoribus in hac tanta occupatione urbis ac vitae, nihil ut eis putem licere nescire, quamquam vis oratoris professioque ipsa bene dicendi hoc suscipere ac polliceri videtur, ut omni de re, quaecumque sit proposita, ornate ab eo copioseque dicatur. . . .

Aut tam iucundum cognitu atque auditu, quam sapientibus sententiis gravibusque verbis ornata oratio et polita? Aut tam potens tamque magnificum, quam populi motus, iudicum religiones, senatus gravitatem unius oratione converti? Quid tam porro regium, tam liberale, tam munificum, quam opem ferre supplicibus, excitare adflictos, dare salutem, liberare periculis, retinere homines in civitate? . . .

Vt vero iam ad illa summa veniamus, quae vis alia potuit aut dispersos homines unum in locum congregare aut a fera agrestique vita ad hunc humanum cultum civilemque deducere aut iam constitutis civitatibus leges iudicia iura describere? Ac ne plura, quae sunt paene innumerabilia, consecter, comprehendam brevi: sic enim statuo, perfecti oratoris moderatione et sapientia non solum ipsius dignitatem, sed et privatorum plurimorum et universae rei publicae salutem maxime contineri.

COMPROMISE

On the State 3.23: Cum autem certi propter divitias aut genus aut aliquas opes rem publicam tenent, est factio, sed vocantur illi optimates. Si vero populus plurimum potest omniaque eius arbitrio reguntur, dicitur illa libertas, est vero licentia. Sed cum alius alium timet, et homo hominem et ordo ordinem, tum quia sibi nemo confidit, quasi pactio fit inter populum et potentis.

Letter to Lentulus Spinther 1.9.11, 21: Ego si ab improbis et perditis civibus rem publicam teneri viderem, sicut et Cinneis temporibus scimus et non nullis aliis accidisse, non modo praemiis, quae apud me minimum valent, sed ne periculis quidem compulsus ullis, quibus tamen moventur etiam fortissimi viri, ad eorum causam me adiungerem, ne si summa quidem eorum in me merita constarent. Cum autem in re publica Cn. Pompeius princeps esset vir, is qui hanc potentiam et gloriam maximis in rem publicam meritis praestantissimisque rebus gestis esset consecutus, cuiusque ego dignitatis ab adulescentia fautor, in praetura autem et in consulatu adiutor etiam exstitissem, cumque idem auctoritate et sententia per se, consiliis et studiis tecum me adiuvisset meumque inimicum unum in civitate haberet inimicum, non putavi famam inconstantiae mihi pertimescendam, si quibusdam in sententiis paulum me inmutassem meamque voluntatem ad summi viri de meque optime meriti dignitatem adgregassem. . . .

Accepisti, quibus rebus adductus quamque
rem causamque defenderim, quique meus in re
publica sit pro mea parte capessenda status. De
quo sic velim statuas, me haec eadem sensurum
fuisse, si mihi integra omnia ac libera fuissent;
nam neque pugnandum arbitrarer contra tantas
opes neque delendum, etiam si id fieri posset,
summorum civium principatum neque per-
manendum in una sententia conversis rebus ac
bonorum voluntatibus mutatis, sed temporibus
adsentiendum. Numquam enim in praestanti-
bus in re publica gubernanda viris laudata est
in una sententia perpetua permansio, sed, ut in
enavigando tempestati obsequi artis est, etiam
si portum tenere non queas, cum vero id possis
mutata velificatione adsequi, stultum est eum
tenere cum periculo cursum, quem coeperis,
potius quam eo commutato quo velis tamen
pervenire, sic, cum omnibus nobis in admi-
nistranda re publica propositum esse debeat, id

quod a me saepissime dictum est, cum dignitate
otium, non idem semper dicere, sed idem semper spectare debemus.

Letter to Atticus 7.1.2–4: Per fortunas, omnem
tuum amorem quo me es amplexus omnem-
que tuam prudentiam quam me hercule in
omni genere iudico singularem confer ad eam
curam ut de omni statu meo cogites. Videre
enim mihi videor tantam dimicationem, nisi
idem deus qui nos melius quam optare au-
deremus Parthico bello liberavit respexerit
rem publicam,—sed tantam quanta numquam
fuit. Age, hoc malum mihi commune est cum
omnibus. Nihil tibi mando ut de eo cogites,
illud meum proprium πρόβλημα, quaeso,
suscipe. videsne ut te auctore sim utrumque
complexus? ac vellem a principio te audisse
amicissime monentem, ἀλλ᾽ ἐμὸν οὔποτε θυμὸν ἐνὶ

στήθεσσιν ἔπειθες. Sed aliquando tamen persua-
sisti ut alterum complecterer quia de me erat
optime meritus, alterum quia tantum valebat.
Feci igitur itaque effeci omni obsequio ut
neutri illorum quisquam esset me carior. Haec
enim cogitabamus, nec mihi coniuncto cum
Pompeio fore necesse peccare in re publica
aliquando nec cum Caesare sentienti pugnandum esse cum Pompeio. Tanta erat illorum
coniunctio. Nunc impendet, ut et tu ostendis
et ego video, summa inter eos contentio.
Me autem uterque numerat suum, nisi forte
simulat alter. Nam Pompeius non dubitat; vere
enim iudicat ea quae de re publica nunc sentiat
mihi valde probari. Vtriusque autem accepi
eius modi litteras eodem tempore quo tuas, ut
neuter quemquam omnium pluris facere quam
me videretur. Verum quid agam? . . . Non est
locus ad tergiversandum.

MONEY AND POWER

On Duties 2.72–78: Ut etiam singulis consulatur, sed ita, ut ea res aut prosit aut certe ne obsit rei publicae. C. Gracchi frumentaria magna largitio; exhauriebat igitur aerarium; modica M. Octavi et rei publicae tolerabilis et plebi necessaria; ergo et civibus et rei publicae salutaris.

In primis autem videndum erit ei, qui rem publicam administrabit, ut suum quisque teneat neque de bonis privatorum publice deminutio fiat. Perniciose enim Philippus, in tribunatu cum legem agrariam ferret, quam tamen antiquari facile passus est et in eo vehementer se moderatum praebuit—sed cum in agendo multa populariter, tum illud male, "non esse in civitate duo milia hominum, qui rem haberent." Capitalis oratio est, ad aequationem bonorum pertinens; qua peste quae potest esse maior? Hanc enim ob causam maxime, ut sua tenerentur, res publicae civitatesque constitutae sunt. Nam, etsi duce natura congregabantur hominess, tamen spe custodiae rerum suarum urbium praesidia quaerebant.

Danda etiam opera est, ne, quod apud maiores nostros saepe fiebat propter aerarii tenuitatem assiduitatemque bellorum, tributum sit conferendum, idque ne eveniat, multo ante erit providendum. Sin quae necessitas huius muneris alicui rei publicae obvenerit (malo enim quam nostrae ominari; neque tamen de nostra, sed de omni re publica disputo), danda erit opera, ut omnes intellegant, si salvi esse velint, necessitati esse parendum. Atque etiam omnes, qui rem publicam gubernabunt, consulere debebunt, ut earum rerum copia sit, quae sunt necessariae. Quarum qualis comparatio fieri soleat et debeat, non est necesse disputare; est enim in promptu; tantum locus attingendus fuit.

Caput autem est in omni procuratione negotii et muneris publici, ut avaritiae pellatur etiam minima suspicio. "Utinam," inquit C. Pontius Samnis, "ad illa tempora me fortuna reservavisset et tum essem natus, quando Romani dona accipere coepissent! Non essem passus diutius eos imperare." Ne illi multa saecula exspectanda fuerunt; modo enim hoc malum in hanc rem publicam invasit. Itaque facile patior tum potius Pontium fuisse, siquidem in illo tantum fuit roboris. Nondum centum et decem anni sunt, cum de pecuniis repetundis a L. Pisone lata lex est, nulla antea cum fuisset. At vero postea tot leges et proximae quaeque duriores, tot rei, tot damnati, tantum Italicum bellum propter iudiciorum metum excitatum, tanta sublatis legibus et iudiciis expilatio direptioque sociorum, ut imbecillitate aliorum, non nostra virtute valeamus.

Laudat Africanum Panaetius, quod fuerit abstinens. Quidni laudet? Sed in illo alia maiora; laus abstinentiae non hominis est solum, sed etiam temporum illorum. Omni Macedonum gaza, quae fuit maxima, potitus est Paulus tantum in aerarium pecuniae invexit, ut unius imperatoris praeda finem attulerit tributorum. At hic nihil domum suam intulit praeter memoriam nominis sempiternam. Imitatus patrem Africanus nihilo locupletior Carthagine eversa. Quid? Qui eius collega fuit in censura. L. Mummius, numquid copiosior, cum copiosissimam urbem funditus sustulisset? Italiam ornare quam domum suam maluit; quamquam Italia ornata domus ipsa mihi videtur ornatior.

Nullum igitur vitium taetrius est, ut eo, unde egressa est, referat se oratio, quam avaritia, praesertim in principibus et rem publicam gubernantibus. Habere enim quaestui rem publicam non modo turpe est, sed sceleratum etiam et nefarium. Itaque, quod Apollo Pythius oraclum edidit, Spartam nulla re alia nisi avaritia esse perituram, id videtur non solum Lacedaemoniis, sed etiam omnibus opulentis populis praedixisse. Nulla autem re conciliare facilius benivolentiam multitudinis possunt ii, qui rei publicae praesunt, quam abstinentia et continentia.

Qui vero se populares volunt ob eamque causam aut agrariam rem temptant, ut possessores pellantur suis sedibus, aut pecunias creditas debitoribus condonandas putant, labefactant fundamenta rei publicae, concordiam primum, quae esse non potest, cum aliis adimuntur, aliis condonantur pecuniae, deinde aequitatem, quae tollitur omnis, si habere suum cuique non licet. Id enim est proprium, ut supra dixi, civitatis atque urbis, ut sit libera et non sollicita suae rei cuiusque custodia.

Against Verres 5.126: Patimur enim multos annos et silemus, cum videamus ad paucos homines omnis omnium nationum pecunias pervenisse. Quod eo magis ferre animo aequo et concedere videamur, quia nemo istorum dissimulat, nemo laborat ut obscura sua cupiditas esse videatur.

Immigration

In Defense of Balbus 22, 24, 30, 31: Atqui si imperatoribus nostris, si senatui, si populo Romano non licebit propositis praemiis elicere ex civitatibus sociorum atque amicorum fortissimum atque optimum quemque ad subeunda pro salutate nostra pericula, summa utilitate ac maximo saepe praesidio periculosis atque asperis temporibus carendum nobis erit. . . .

Nam stipendiarios ex Africa, Sicilia, Sardinia, ceteris provinciis multos civitate donatos videmus, et, qui hostes ad nostros imperatores perfugissent et magno usui rei publicae nostrae fuissent, scimus civitate esse donatos; servos denique, quorum ius, fortuna, condicio infima est, bene de re publica meritos persaepe libertate, id est civitate, publice donari videmus. . . .

Defendo enim rem universam, nullam esse gentem ex omni regione terrarum, neque tam dissidentem a populo Romano odio quodam atque discidio, neque tam fide benivolentiaque coniunctam, ex qua nobis interdictum sit ne quem adsciscere civem aut civitate donare possimus. . . .

Illud vero sine ulla dubitatione maxime nostrum fundavit imperium et populi Romani nomen auxit, quod princeps ille creator huius urbis, Romulus, foedere Sabino docuit etiam hostibus recipiendis augeri hanc civitatem oportere; cuius auctoritate et exemplo numquam est intermissa a maioribus nostris largitio et communicatio civitatis.

WAR

For the Manlian Law 11–12: Maiores nostri saepe pro mercatoribus aut naviculariis nostris iniuriosius tractatis bella gesserunt; vos tot milibus civium Romanorum uno nuntio atque uno tempore necatis quo tandem animo esse debetis? Legati quod erant appellati superbius, Corinthum patres vestri totius Graeciae lumen exstinctum esse voluerunt; vos eum regem inultum esse patiemini qui legatum populi Romani consularem vinculis ac verberibus atque omni supplicio excruciatum necavit? Illi libertatem imminutam civium Romanorum non tulerunt; vos ereptam vitam neglegetis? Ius legationis verbo violatum illi persecuti sunt; vos legatum omni supplicio interfectum relinquetis? Videte ne, ut illis pulcherrimum fuit tantam vobis imperi gloriam tradere, sic vobis turpissimum sit id quod accepistis tueri et conservare non posse.

On the State 3.34–35: Nullum bellum suscipi a civitate optima nisi aut pro fide aut pro salute. . . .

Illa iniusta bella sunt, quae sunt sine causa suscepta. Nam extra ulciscendi aut propulsandorum hostium causam bellum geri iustum nullum potest. . . .

Nullum bellum iustum habetur nisi denuntiatum, nisi indictum, nisi repetitis rebus. . . .

Corruption

Against Verres 5.1, 27–28, 63–64, 183: Nemini video dubium esse, iudices, quin apertissime C. Verres in Sicilia sacra profanaque omnia et privatim et publice spoliarit, versatusque sit sine ulla non modo religione verum etiam dissimulatione in omni genere furandi atque praedandi. . . .

Cum autem ver esse coeperat—cuius initium iste non a Favonio neque ab aliquo astro notabat, sed cum rosam viderat tum incipere ver arbitrabatur—dabat se labori atque itineribus; in quibus eo usque se praebebat patientem atque impigrum ut eum nemo umquam in equo sedentem viderit. Nam, ut mos fuit Bithyniae regibus, lectica octaphoro ferebatur, in qua pulvinus erat perlucidus Melitensis rosa fartus; ipse autem coronam habebat unam in capite, alteram in collo, reticulumque ad naris sibi admovebat tenuissimo lino, minutis maculis, plenum rosae. Sic confecto itinere cum ad aliquod oppidum venerat, eadem lectica usque in cubiculum deferebatur. Eo veniebant Siculorum magistratus, veniebant equites Romani, id quod ex multis iuratis audistis; controversiae secreto deferebantur, paulo post palam decreta auferebantur. Deinde ubi paulisper in cubiculo pretio non aequitate iura discripserat, Veneri iam et Libero reliquum tempus deberi arbitrabatur. Quo loco non mihi praetermittenda videtur praeclari imperatoris egregia ac singularis diligentia. Nam scitote oppidum esse in Sicilia nullum ex iis oppidis in quibus consistere praetores et conventum agere soleant, quo in oppido non isti ex aliqua familia non ignobili delecta ad libidinem mulier esset. Itaque non nullae ex eo numero in convivium adhibebantur palam; si quae castiores erant, ad tempus veniebant, lucem conventumque vitabant. erant autem convivia non illo silentio populi Romani praetorum atque imperatorum, neque eo pudore qui in magistratuum conviviis versari soleat, sed cum maximo clamore atque convicio; non numquam etiam res ad pugnam atque ad manus vocabatur. Iste enim praetor severus ac diligens, qui populi Romani legibus numquam paruisset, illis legibus quae in poculis ponebantur diligenter obtemperabat. Itaque erant exitus eius modi ut alius inter manus e convivio tamquam e proelio auferretur, alius tamquam occisus relinqueretur, plerique ut fusi sine mente ac sine ullo sensu iacerent,—ut quivis, cum aspexisset, non se praetoris convivium, sed Cannensem pugnam nequitiae videre arbitraretur. . . .

Cum propter istius hanc avaritiam nomine classis esset in Sicilia, re quidem vera naves inanes, quae praedam praetori non quae

praedonibus metum adferrent, tamen, cum
P. Caesetius et P. Tadius decem navibus suis
semiplenis navigarent, navem quandam pirata-
rum praeda refertam non ceperunt, sed abdux-
erunt onere suo plane captam atque depressam.
Erat ea navis plena iuventutis formosissimae,
plena argenti facti atque signati, multa cum
stragula veste. Haec una navis a classe nostra
non capta est, sed inventa ad Megaridem, qui
locus est non longe a Syracusis. Quod ubi isti
nuntiatum est, tametsi in acta cum muliercu-
lis iacebat ebrius, erexit se tamen et statim
quaestori legatoque suo custodes misit com-
pluris, ut omnia sibi integra quam primum
exhiberentur. Adpellitur navis Syracusas;
exspectatur ab omnibus supplicium. iste quasi
praeda sibi advecta, non praedonibus captis,
si qui senes ac deformes erant, eos in hostium
numero ducit; qui aliquid formae aetatis arti-
ficique habebant, abducit omnis, non nullos

scribis filio cohortique distribuit, symphoniacos homines sex cuidam amico suo Romam muneri misit. Nox illa tota in exinaniunda nave consumitur. . . .

Quam ob rem mihi, iudices, optatum illud est, in hoc reo finem accusandi facere, cum et populo Romano satis factum et receptum officium Siculis, necessariis meis, erit persolutum; deliberatum autem est, si res opinionem meam quam de vobis habeo fefellerit, non modo eos persequi ad quos maxime culpa corrupti iudici, sed etiam illos ad quos conscientiae contagio pertinebit. Proinde si qui sunt qui in hoc reo aut potentes aut audaces ant artifices ad corrumpendum iudicium velint esse, ita sint parati ut disceptante populo Romano mecum sibi rem videant futuram; et si me in hoc reo, quem mihi inimicum Siculi dederunt, satis vehementem, satis perseverantem, satis vigilantem esse cognorunt, existiment in iis hominibus quorum ego inimicitias populi Romani salutis causa suscepero multo graviorem atque acriorem futurum.

TYRANNY

On Duties 2.22–24: Atque etiam subiciunt se homines imperio alterius et potestati de causis pluribus. Ducuntur enim aut benivolentia aut beneficiorum magnitudine aut dignitatis praestantia aut spe sibi id utile futurum aut metu ne vi parere cogantur, aut spe largitionis promissisque capti aut postremo, ut saepe in nostra re publica videmus, mercede conducti.

Omnium autem rerum nec aptius est quicquam ad opes tuendas ac tenendas quam diligi nec alienius quam timeri. Praeclare enim Ennius: Quem metuunt, oderunt; quem quisque odit, periisse expetit. Multorum autem odiis nullas opes posse obsistere, si antea fuit ignotum, nuper est cognitum. Nec vero huius tyranni solum, quem armis oppressa pertulit civitas ac paret cum maxime mortuo, interitus declarat, quantum odium hominum valeat ad pestem, sed reliquorum similes exitus tyrannorum, quorum haud fere quisquam talem interitum effugit; malus enim est custos diuturnitatis metus contraque benivolentia fidelis vel ad perpetuitatem.

Sed iis, qui vi oppressos imperio coercent, sit sane adhibenda saevitia, ut eris in famulos, si aliter teneri non possunt; qui vero in libera civitate ita se instruunt, ut metuantur, iis nihil potest esse dementius. Quamvis enim sint demersae leges alicuius opibus, quamvis timefacta libertas, emergunt tamen haec aliquando aut iudiciis tacitis aut occultis de honore suffragiis. Acriores autem morsus sunt intermissae libertatis quam retentae. Quod igitur latissime patet neque ad incolumitatem solum, sed etiam ad opes et potentiam valet plurimum, id amplectamur, ut metus absit, caritas retineatur. Ita facillime, quae volemus, et privatis in rebus et in re publica consequemur.

On the State 3.43–45:
S. Ergo illam rem populi, id est rem publicam, quis diceret tum, cum crudelitate unius oppressi essent universi, neque esset unum vinculum iuris nec consensus ac societas coetus, quod est populus? Atque hoc idem Syracusis. Urbs illa praeclara, quam ait Timaeus Graecarum maxumam, omnium autem esse pulcherrimam, arx visenda, portus usque in sinus oppidi et ad urbis crepidines infusi, viae latae, porticus, templa, muri nihilo magis efficiebant, Dionysio tenente ut esset illa res publica; nihil enim populi et unius erat populus ipse. Ergo ubi tyrannus est,

ibi non vitiosam, ut heri dicebam, sed, ut nunc ratio cogit, dicendum est plane nullam esse rem publicam.

L. Praeclare quidem dicis; etenim video iam, quo pergat oratio.

S. Vides igitur ne illam quidem, quae tota sit in factionis potestate, posse vere dici rem publicam.

L. Sic plane iudico.

S. Et rectissime quidem iudicas; quae enim fuit tum Atheniensium res, cum post magnum illud Peloponnesiacum bellum triginta viri illi urbi iniustissime praefuerunt? Num aut vetus gloria civitatis aut species praeclara oppidi aut theatrum, gymnasia, porticus aut propylaea nobilia aut arx aut admiranda opera Phidiae aut Piraeus ille magnificus rem publicam efficiebat?

L. Minime vero, quoniam quidem populi res non erat.

S. Quid? Cum decemviri Romae sine pro-
vocatione fuerunt tertio illo anno, cum vindi-
cias amisisset ipsa libertas?

L. Populi nulla res erat, immo vero id
populus egit, ut rem suam recuperaret.

S. Venio nunc ad tertium genus illud, in
quo esse videbuntur fortasse angustiae. Cum
per populum agi dicuntur et esse in populi
potestate omnia, cum, de quocumque volt, supplicium sumit multitudo, cum agunt, rapiunt,
tenent, dissipant, quae volunt, potesne tum,
Laeli, negare rem esse illam publicam, cum populi sint omnia, quoniam quidem populi esse
rem volumus rem publicam?

L. Ac nullam quidem citius negaverim esse
rem publicam, quam istam, quae tota plane sit
in multitudinis potestate. Nam si nobis non
placuit Syracusis fuisse rem publicam neque
Agrigenti neque Athenis, cum essent tyranni,

nec hic, cum decemviri; nec video, qui magis in multitudinis dominatu rei publicae nomen appareat, quia primum mihi populus non est, ut tu optime definisti, Scipio, nisi qui consensu iuris continetur, sed est tam tyrannus iste conventus, quam si esset unus, hoc etiam taetrior, quia nihil ista, quae populi speciem et nomen imitatur.

Philippics 2.117–19: Cum illo ego te dominandi cupiditate conferre possum, ceteris vero rebus nullo modo comparandus es. Sed ex plurimis malis quae ab illo rei publicae sunt inusta hoc tamen boni est quod didicit iam populus Romanus quantum cuique crederet, quibus se committeret, a quibus caveret. Haec non cogitas, neque intellegis satis esse viris fortibus didicisse quam sit re pulchrum, beneficio gratum, fama gloriosum tyrannum occidere? An, cum illum

homines non tulerint, te ferent? Certatim posthac, mihi crede, ad hoc opus curretur neque
occasionis tarditas exspectabitur.

Respice, quaeso, aliquando rem publicam,
M. Antoni, quibus ortus sis, non quibuscum
vivas considera: mecum, ut voles: redi cum re
publica in gratiam. Sed de te tu videris; ego
de me ipse profitebor. defendi rem publicam
adulescens, non deseram senex: contempsi
Catilinae gladios, non pertimescam tuos. Quin
etiam corpus libenter obtulerim, si reprae-
sentari morte mea libertas civitatis potest, ut
aliquando dolor populi Romani pariat quod
iam diu parturit! etenim si abhinc annos prope
viginti hoc ipso in templo negavi posse mor-
tem immaturam esse consulari, quanto verius
nunc negabo seni? Mihi vero, patres conscripti,
iam etiam optanda mors est, perfuncto rebus
eis quas adeptus sum quasque gessi. Duo
modo haec opto, unum ut moriens populum

Romanum liberum relinquam—hoc mihi maius
ab dis immortalibus dari nihil potest—alterum
ut ita cuique eveniat ut de re publica quisque
mereatur.

Cicero's Epilogue: The Fallen State

On the State 5.1–2:

> Moribus antiquis res stat Romana virisque.
>
> —Ennius, *Annales*

Quem quidem ille versum vel brevitate vel
veritate tamquam ex oraculo mihi quodam
esse effatus videtur. Nam neque viri, nisi ita
morata civitas fuisset, neque mores, nisi hi viri
praefuissent, aut fundare aut tam diu tenere po-
tuissent tantam et tam fuse lateque imperantem
rem publicam. Itaque ante nostram memoriam
et mos ipse patrius praestantes viros adhibebat,

et veterem morem ac maiorum instituta retine-
bant excellentes viri. Nostra vero aetas cum rem
publicam sicut picturam accepisset egregiam,
sed iam evanescentem vetustate, non modo
eam coloribus eisdem, quibus fuerat, renovare
neglexit, sed ne id quidem curavit, ut formam
saltem eius et extrema tamquam liniamenta ser-
varet. Quid enim manet ex antiquis moribus,
quibus ille dixit rem stare Romanam? Quos ita
oblivione obsoletos videmus, ut non modo non
colantur, sed iam ignorentur. Nam de viris quid
dicam? Mores enim ipsi interierunt virorum
penuria, cuius tanti mali non modo reddenda
ratio nobis, sed etiam tamquam reis capitis
quodam modo dicenda causa est. Nostris enim
vitiis, non casu aliquo, rem publicam verbo
retinemus, re ipsa vero iam pridem amisimus.

PASSAGES TRANSLATED

Natural Law: *On the State* 3.33 (by permission of
  Oxford University Press, www.oup.com: from *M.
  Tulli Ciceronis: De Re Publica, De Legibus, Cato
  Maior de Senectute, Laelius de Amicitia*, ed. J.G.F.
  Powell, Oxford University Press, 2006, pp. 107–8);
  On Laws 3.2–3 (by permission of Oxford University
  Press, www.oup.com: from *M. Tulli Ciceronis: De Re
  Publica, De Legibus, Cato Maior de Senectute, Lae-
  lius de Amicitia*, ed. J.G.F. Powell, Oxford University
  Press, 2006, pp. 237–38).
Balance of Power: *On the State* 1.69 33 (by permission
  of Oxford University Press, www.oup.com: from
  *M. Tulli Ciceronis: De Re Publica, De Legibus, Cato
  Maior de Senectute, Laelius de Amicitia*, ed. J.G.F.
  Powell, Oxford University Press, 2006, pp. 48–49).
Leadership: *Letter to Quintus* 1.1.4–5 (by permission of
  Oxford University Press, www.oup.com: from *M.
  Tulli Ciceronis: Epistulae*, vol. 3, ed. L. Purser, Oxford
  University Press, 1953, pp. 2–3); *In Defense of Sestius*
  98–100 (by permission of Oxford University Press,
  www.oup.com: from *M. Tulli Ciceronis: Orationes*,

from *M. Tulli Ciceronis: Rhetorica*, ed. A. S. Wilkins, Oxford University Press, 1963, four pages of text not numbered.).

Compromise: *On the State* 3.23 (by permission of Oxford University Press, www.oup.com: from *M. Tulli Ciceronis: De Re Publica, De Legibus, Cato Maior de Senectute, Laelius de Amicitia*, ed. J.G.F. Powell, Oxford University Press, 2006, p. 103.); *Letter to Lentulus Spinther* 1.9.11, 21 (by permission of Oxford University Press, www.oup.com: from *M. Tulli Ciceronis: Epistulae*, ed. L. Purser, Oxford University Press, 1952, three pages of text not numbered); *Letter to Atticus* 7.1.2–4 (by permission of Oxford University Press, www.oup.com: from *M. Tulli Ciceronis: Epistulae*, vol. 2, ed. L. Purser, Oxford University Press, 1952, three pages of text not numbered).

Money and Power: *On Duties* 2.72–78 (reprinted by permission of the publishers and the Trustees of the Loeb Classical Library from *Cicero: Volume XXI*, Loeb Classical Library Volume 30, trans. Walter Miller, Cambridge, Mass.: Harvard University Press, 1913, pp. 246–54. Loeb Classical Library (R) is a registered trademark of the President and Fellows of Harvard College); *Against Verres* 5.126 (by permission of Oxford University Press, www.oup.com: from *M. Tulli Ciceronis: Orationes*, ed. G. Peterson, Oxford University Press, 1965, one page of text not numbered).

PASSAGES TRANSLATED

Immigration: *In Defense of Balbus* 22, 24, 30, 31 (by permission of Oxford University Press, www.oup.com: from *M. Tulli Ciceronis: Orationes*, ed. G. Peterson, Oxford University Press, 1962), two pages of text not numbered).

War: *For the Manlian Law* 11–12 (by permission of Oxford University Press, www.oup.com: from *M. Tulli Ciceronis: Orationes*, ed. A. Clark, Oxford University Press, 1965, one page of text not numbered); *On the State* 3.34–35 (by permission of Oxford University Press, www.oup.com: from *M. Tulli Ciceronis: De Re Publica, De Legibus, Cato Maior de Senectute, Laelius de Amicitia*, ed. J.G.F. Powell, Oxford University Press, 2006, p. 107).

Corruption: *Against Verres* 5.1, 27–28, 63–64, 183 (by permission of Oxford University Press, www.oup .com: from *M. Tulli Ciceronis: Orationes*, ed. G. Peterson, Oxford University Press, 1965, seven pages of text not numbered).

Tyranny: *On Duties* 2.22–24 (reprinted by permission of the publishers and the Trustees of the Loeb Classical Library from *Cicero: Volume XXI*, Loeb Classical Library Volume 30, trans. Walter Miller, Cambridge, Mass.: Harvard University Press, 1913, pp. 188–92. Loeb Classical Library (R) is a registered trademark of the President and Fellows of Harvard College); *On the State* 3.43–45 (by permission of Oxford University Press, www.oup.com: from *M. Tulli*

PASSAGES TRANSLATED

Ciceronis: De Re Publica, De Legibus, Cato Maior de Senectute, Laelius de Amicitia, ed. J.G.F. Powell, Oxford University Press, 2006, pp. 111–13); *Philippics* 2.117–19 (by permission of Oxford University Press, www.oup.com: from *M. Tulli Ciceronis: Orationes*, ed. A. Clark, Oxford University Press, 1963, one page of text not numbered).

Cicero's Epilogue: The Fallen State: On the State 5.1–2 (by permission of Oxford University Press, www .oup.com: from *M. Tulli Ciceronis: De Re Publica, De Legibus, Cato Maior de Senectute, Laelius de Amicitia*, ed. J.G.F. Powell, Oxford University Press, 2006, pp. 127–28).

GLOSSARY

AGRIGENTUM: A Greek city of southern Sicily ruled by tyrants until democracy was established.

ALLOBROGES: A Celtic tribe of southeastern Gaul who helped Cicero reveal the conspiracy of Catiline in 63 BC, though they revolted against Rome two years later.

ARPINUM: Home of Marcus Cicero, it was a hilltown originally of the Volscians southeast of Rome whose inhabitants were given full Roman citizenship in 188 BC.

ATTICUS: Titus Pomponius Atticus, wealthy boyhood companion of Marcus Cicero who remained his confidant and friend throughout his life. Cicero's surviving letters to Atticus are one of the best sources for his life and times.

BACCHUS: (Liber) Roman name for Dionysus, Greek god of wine and revelry.

BALBUS: Lucius Cornelius Balbus, he was born in Iberian Gades (Cádiz) and won Roman citizenship in 72 BC with the help of Pompey. He was prosecuted in 56 BC for gaining citizenship illegally and was successfully defended by Marcus Cicero. He became a loyal supporter of Julius Caesar and later of Octavian. In 40 BC he became Rome's first foreign-born consul.

GLOSSARY

BITHYNIA: An agriculturally rich kingdom and later Roman province in northwest Asia Minor known for, among other luxuries, its litter-bearers.

BOARD OF TEN: Latin *decemviri*, in Roman tradition two groups of ten men who met in 451 and 450 BC to draw up a set of law codes. The second group became tyrannical and refused to yield power until forced from office.

CAESAR: Gaius Julius Caesar, born 100 BC, a nobleman who rose to political power and through his military skills conquered Gaul for Rome. He crossed the Rubicon River in 49 BC and started a civil war with his former partner Pompey and the republican leadership. He defeated them and set himself up as dictator for life until he was murdered, on the Ides of March, 44 BC.

CANNAE: Site in southern Italy where the Romans were defeated by Hannibal in 216 BC, when the Carthaginian general killed tens of thousands of Roman soldiers in one of the greatest battlefield massacres in history.

CARTHAGE: Prosperous city in north Africa founded by Phoenicians, it became a powerful commercial and military rival of Rome until it was finally destroyed in 146 BC.

CATILINE: Lucius Sergius Catilina, a patrician who was defeated by Marcus Cicero for consul in 64 BC. He fomented an insurrection against Rome the next year but was exposed and defeated thanks in large part to Cicero.

CATO: Marcus Porcius Cato, a younger contemporary of Marcus Cicero, was a stalwart defender of Roman republican traditions. He fought against Julius Caesar and committed suicide in 46 BC after his defeat.

CINNA: Lucius Cornelius Cinna, an aristocrat who nonetheless worked against senatorial power and opposed the Roman general Sulla. He was consul three years in a row (86–84 BC), but was murdered in a mutiny while preparing to fight against Sulla.

CLODIUS: Publius Clodius Pulcher, a patrician turned populist plebeian who scandalized Rome when he dressed as a woman to attended the female-only *Bona Dea* rites in 62 BC. He became an implacable enemy of Cicero until he was murdered by an opposing faction in 52 BC.

CONSUL: The highest office in the Roman Republic. There were two consuls elected annually to serve a one-year term.

CORINTH: Prosperous Greek city on the isthmus connecting the Peloponnese to central Greece. It was destroyed in 146 BC but was rebuilt.

CRASSUS: Marcus Licinius Crassus, wealthy ally of Pompey and Julius Caesar who was killed by the Parthians in 53 BC.

DELPHI: Oracle of Apollo in central Greece.

DIONYSIUS: Wealthy and powerful tyrant of the Sicilian city of Syracuse in the early fourth century BC.

ENNIUS: Quintus Ennius (239–169 BC), an immigrant to Rome from southern Italy, was one of the earliest Latin writers. He composed prose, plays, and a poetic history of Rome known as the *Annales*.

GADES: Modern Cádiz, a Phoenician colony on the western coast of the Iberian peninsula and home of Balbus, whom Cicero defended.

GAIUS GRACCHUS: Gaius Sempronius Gracchus, along with his brother Tiberius, attempted radical political reformation of the Roman Republic in the late second century BC.

GAIUS PONTIUS: Gaius or Gavius Pontius was a Samnite general who reportedly entrapped and defeated a Roman army in 321 BC at the Caudine Forks. He had a reputation for great wisdom in Roman tradition.

GAIUS VERRES: Notorious Roman governor of Sicily in 73–71 BC who was prosecuted by Cicero for exploiting the province and fled with his ill-gotten gains into exile at Massalia in Gaul.

GAUL: Roughly modern France, it was conquered by Julius Caesar in 58–50 BC.

GOOD GODDESS: *Bona Dea* in Latin, an Italian goddess who was worshipped in Rome annually in a ceremony attended exclusively by women. Clodius defiled her worship in 62 BC when he snuck into the celebration dressed as a woman.

HOMER: Eighth-century BC Greek poet who composed the *Iliad* and *Odyssey*.

LAELIUS: Gaius Laelius, second-century BC Roman conservative politician and friend of Scipio. He serves as a central character in two of Cicero's philosophical dialogues.

LENTULUS SPINTHER: Publius Cornelius Lentulus Spinther, consul in 57 BC and friend of Cicero who helped return him from exile and regain his lost property.

LILYBAEUM: Modern Marsala, a city in western Sicily developed by the Carthaginians and used by the Romans as a base for one of its provincial quaestors. Cicero served there in 75 BC.

LUCIUS MUMMIUS: Consul in 146 BC who defeated an uprising in Greece and destroyed the city of Corinth.

LUCIUS PISO: Lucius Calpurnius Piso Frugi ("the frugal") served as tribune in 149 BC, then consul in 133, and was known for his stand against greed and corruption.

LYCURGUS: Traditional founder of Sparta's strict military and political institutions.

MACEDONIA: Kingdom of Philip II and Alexander the Great in the northern Balkans, it was conquered by the Romans in 167 BC and in 146 BC became a Roman province.

MALTA: The island known in Roman times as Melita, an important trading center between Italy and Africa.

MARCUS OCTAVIUS: Tribune in 133 BC who opposed the reforms of Tiberius Gracchus and was deposed.

MARK ANTONY: Marcus Antonius, who served under Julius Caesar in Gaul, then supported him in the civil war that followed. After the assassination of Caesar in 44 BC, he worked with and then fought against Octavian for control of Rome. Cicero denounced him in a series of speeches known as the *Philippics* and was murdered soon after at Antony's behest.

MEGARA HYBLAEA: Greek city on the east coast of Sicily destroyed by the Romans in 213 BC.

METELLUS CELER: Quintus Caecilius Metellus Celer, praetor in 63 BC, he commanded the forces against the conspirators of Catiline.

MITHRADATES: Mithradates VI Eupator Dionysus, king of Pontus in northern Asia Minor, enemy of Rome for decades, he massacred many Roman and Italian residents of Asia Minor in his war against Rome beginning in 89 BC.

NATURAL LAW: The belief that certain principles are rooted in nature and so are universally valid.

OCTAVIAN: Gaius Octavius, later the emperor Augustus, was born in 63 BC, the year of Cicero's consulship. As great-nephew and heir of Julius Caesar, he rose to power as a young man first as a partner and then as the opponent of Mark Antony.

PANAETIUS: Stoic philosopher of the second century BC who moved to Rome and became part of the circle of Scipio.

PARTHIA: The powerful Parthian Empire stretched from India to the eastern borders of Roman territory and was Rome's chief military rival in the time of Cicero.

PAULLUS: Lucius Aemilius Paullus, victorious Roman general in the Third Macedonian War in 168 BC.

GLOSSARY

Peloponnesian War: A long and devastating conflict fought from 431–401 BC between Athens and Sparta.

Phidias: Famous and influential fifth-century BC Athenian sculptor.

Piraeus: The ancient (and modern) port of Athens.

Piso: Lucius Calpurnius Piso Caesoninus, consul in 58 BC and opponent of Cicero in favor of Clodius.

Pompey: Gnaeus Pompeius Magnus ("the Great"), successful Roman general and patron of Cicero who at first allied himself with Julius Caesar and then fought against him.

pontiff: A member of the college of Roman priests.

proconsul: A former Roman consul appointed to serve as a governor of a province.

Propylaea: A monumental roofed gateway, most famously the elaborate fifth-century entrance to the acropolis of Athens.

Publius Sestius: Roman senator and tribune who worked for Cicero's restoration from exile.

Puteoli: Modern Pozzuoli, a fashionable resort north of Naples where many of the Roman elite owned villas.

quaestor: Junior Roman magistrates who served in a number of financial and administrative roles.

Quintus Cicero: Quintus Tullius Cicero, younger brother of Marcus Cicero, who served as governor in the Roman province of Asia from 61–58 BC.

GLOSSARY

REPUBLIC: In Latin, *res publica*, or "property of the people." The Roman Republic was established ca. 500 BC and survived until the rise of the Empire in the late first century BC.

ROMULUS: Legendary founder of Rome who organized a kidnapping of young Sabine women as wives for his settlers.

SABINES: Italic people who lived just to the east of Rome. They were incorporated into the Roman state by the early third century BC.

SAMNITES: Warlike native people of central and southern Italy who fought a long series of wars with the Romans before their final defeat in the first century BC.

SCIPIO: Publius Cornelius Scipio Aemilianus Africanus, noted Roman general and political leader who features prominently as a character in several of Cicero's writings.

SICILY: Large Mediterranean island off the toe of Italy taken over by the Romans in the late third century BC.

SPARTA: City of southern Greece renowned for the toughness of its citizens and its military might.

SYRACUSE: Originally a Greek colony on the eastern coast of Sicily, it became the center of Roman provincial government.

THE THIRTY: Band of thirty Athenian oligarchs who, with Spartan backing, ruled Athens for a little over a year after the end of the Peloponnesian War in 404 BC.

TIMAEUS: Sicilian Greek historian, ca. 350–260 BC.

GLOSSARY

Venus: Roman goddess of love and sex, equivalent to the Greek Aphrodite.

Vestal Virgins: Maiden priestesses of the Roman goddess Vesta who tended her temple in the Roman Forum.

Volscians: Italic people south of Rome who were gradually conquered and assimilated.

FURTHER READING

Bailey, D. R. Shackleton, ed. *Cicero: Selected Letters*. New York: Penguin Books, 1986.

Boatwright, Mary T., Daniel J. Gargola, Noel Lenski, and Richard J. A. Talbert. *The Romans: From Village to Empire*. Oxford: Oxford University Press, 2012.

Everitt, Anthony. *Cicero: The Life and Times of Rome's Greatest Politician*. New York: Random House, 2001.

Freeman, Philip, ed. *How to Win an Election: An Ancient Guide for Modern Politicians*. Princeton, NJ: Princeton University Press, 2012.

Grant, Michael, ed. *Cicero: On Government*. New York: Penguin Books, 1993.

Griffin, M. T., and E. M. Atkins, eds. *Cicero: On Duties*. Cambridge, UK: Cambridge University Press, 1991.

McElduff, Siobhán, ed. *Cicero: In Defense of the Republic*. New York: Penguin Books, 2011.

Rawson, Elizabeth. *Cicero: A Portrait*. London: Bristol Classical Press, 1983.

FURTHER READING

Richard, Carl J. *The Founders and the Classics: Greece, Rome, and the American Enlightenment*. Cambridge, MA: Harvard University Press, 1994.

Walsh, P. G., ed. *Cicero: Selected Letters*. Oxford: Oxford University Press, 2008.

Zetzel, James E. G., ed. *Cicero: On the Commonwealth and On the Laws*. Cambridge, UK: Cambridge University Press, 1999.